"Human services?
. . . That must be so rewarding."

"Human services?
. . . That must be so rewarding."

A Practical Guide for
Professional Development

Second Edition

by

Gail S. Bernstein, Ph.D.
Licensed Psychologist
Denver, Colorado

·P A U L·H·
BROOKES
PUBLISHING C?

Baltimore • London • Toronto • Sydney

Paul H. Brookes Publishing Co.
Post Office Box 10624
Baltimore, Maryland 21285-0624

www.pbrookes.com

Typeset by Barton Matheson Willse & Worthington, Baltimore, Maryland.
Manufactured in the United States of America by
The Maple Press Co., York, Pennsylvania.

With the exception of the 11 people who kindly gave permission for their names and stories to be used, the individuals and situations described in this book are composites based on various people and circumstances. Any similarity to actual individuals or circumstances is coincidental.

Gender specifications alternate throughout the text.

Library of Congress Cataloging-in-Publication Data

Bernstein, Gail S., 1947–
    "Human services? . . . That must be so rewarding." : a practical guide for professional development / by Gail S. Bernstein.
        p.   cm.
    Rev. ed. of: "Human services? . . . That must be so rewarding." / by Gail
S. Bernstein and Judith A. Halaszyn ; [illustrations by Jeff Slemons]. ©1989.
    Includes bibliographical references and index.
    ISBN 1-55766-332-7 (pbk.)
    1. Human services—Vocational guidance.   2. Human services
personnel.   I. Title.
HV10.5.B36   1999
361'.0023'73—dc21   98-36525
                                                                                        CIP

British Library Cataloguing in Publication Data are available from the British
Library.

OCLC# 39539387

She had never been especially impressed by the heroics of the people convinced they are about to change the world. She was more awed by the heroism of those who are willing to struggle to make one small difference after another.

Ellen Goodman
Close to Home

CONTENTS

ABOUT THE AUTHOR

Gail S. Bernstein, Ph.D., Licensed Psychologist, 789 Sherman, Suite 430, Denver, CO 80203-3529

Dr. Bernstein has been working in human services, health care, and education for more than 30 years. Her work with adults of all ages and with adolescents has taken her to group homes, high schools, supported living environments, long-term care facilities, private residential institutions, vocational habilitation programs, inpatient psychiatric hospitals, and outpatient psychotherapy offices.

Dr. Bernstein earned her doctorate in 1978 from the University of Wisconsin–Madison, Department of Studies in Behavioral Disabilities, and is a licensed psychologist in Colorado. Her work includes her psychotherapy practice in Denver, training and consultation for helping professionals, and writing for both general and professional audiences in print and electronic media. She has clinical faculty appointments at the University of Denver School of Professional Psychology and the University of Colorado School of Medicine, Department of Psychiatry.

INTRODUCTION

This book addresses topics that human services professionals usually do not discuss. Most of us are trained in school and/or on the job in methods of providing services. Our training rarely includes consideration of these questions:

- Why do I want to do this?
- What do I expect to get out of it?
- What do I expect to accomplish?
- What values will I use to guide my work?
- How will I act while I provide services?
- How will I manage the stressful aspects of working in human services?

This text is about those questions. The focus here, unlike most human services texts, is clearly on the provider of services rather than on the recipient. This focus is not from any lack of concern for the people who receive our services. Instead, it is the result of my conviction that the most effective and thoughtful services are delivered by people who have clear answers to the questions listed previously.

Chapter 1, On Knowing Yourself, addresses personal motives, goals, and limits for the human services professional. Chapter 2, On Minding Other People's Business, is about client rights and the dignity of the individual. Chapter 3, Human Problems, Human Services Values, suggests fundamental values for the human services. Chapters 4, 5, 6, and 7 cover professional behavior, specifically professional relationships, time management, communication, and professional development. Chapter 8 is about the necessity for and ways to improve self-care and stress management. The closing chapter, The Proactive Human Services Professional, reflects on human services as a career. Throughout the text you will find comments from 11 human services professionals who, in personal interviews, were asked to address the topics covered here. Extended interviews with two of these professionals appear in the closing chapter.

The skills addressed here are complex and difficult to acquire. Each chapter is an introduction to a topic about which many books and scholarly articles have been written. I suggest that you read and work through no more than a chapter per week, taking time to thoroughly consider the questions raised.

My purpose is to provide a book that is, above all, practical and applied rather than academic. Although there are references, no attempt was made to thoroughly examine the vast literature pertaining to the topics covered here. Instead, I relied on a few selected references, some contemporary and some classic; the generosity of colleagues and students in sharing information; and my more than 30 years of experience in human services, health care, and education.

My intended audience consists of people who currently provide or will be providing human services. This includes 1) students in undergraduate and community college programs who are entering practicum programs and 2) people working in any of the human services. Some of the readers who may find this book useful include current and future advocates, child care and youth workers, counselors, developmental disabilities workers, direct services providers, early intervention professionals, geriatrics specialists, independent living center staff, mental health workers, occupational therapists, pastoral counselors, physical therapists, probation officers, psychiatric nurses, psychologists, psychotherapists, rehabilitation personnel, service coordinators, social workers, speech-language pathologists, and teachers.

Sometimes professionals are defined as people who have college degrees, sometimes only those who have graduate degrees. I do not believe in defining professionalism in those ways. Professionalism, in my opinion, is a function of how people behave on the job. Whenever "human services professionals" are referred to in this book, the intent is to include everyone providing human services, regardless of level or type of education.

AND INTRODUCING ...

The reasons human services professionals have for doing what they do and the experiences they have while doing it are every bit as diverse as the services they provide and the people they serve. Eleven of them agreed to talk about the issues addressed in this book. They are

- *Ellen Berlin,* parent educator in schools and childbirth educator in hospitals
- *Suzanne Cardiff,* case aide for a county social services department
- *Heidi Daly,* former social worker in a nursing home, now salesperson and customer service representative for a medical supplies company
- *Jennifer Echarte,* mentor for at-risk adolescents and crisis translator for a community mental health center
- *William Esp,* addictions counselor in an intensive outpatient addictions treatment program at a psychiatric hospital
- *Mary Anne Harvey,* executive director of a protection and advocacy organization serving people with disabilities and older adults
- *Cheryl Lammers,* supervisor of a probation department investigations unit
- *Pamela Meister,* patient advocate in a large teaching hospital
- *Christa Pavlus,* occupational therapist in a long-term care facility for older adults
- *Cathy Phelps,* program director for a victim services center
- *Johnn Young,* prevention outreach coordinator for an AIDS services organization

These nine women and two men range in age from 24 to 49. Two are African American, one is Cuban American, and the remainder are white. One woman identified herself as lesbian, one man identified himself as gay, seven said they are heterosexual, and two did not respond to that item. One interviewee is Christian, one is Episcopalian, one is Lutheran, one is Methodist, one is Pagan, one is Roman Catholic, and five gave no religious affiliation. One person has an associate's degree, six have bachelor's degrees, three have master's degrees, and five have specialized certificates (some have a degree as well as one or more certificates).

Here are nine of their stories about why they chose human services.

Ellen Berlin

I started out in college in recreation and park administration because I decided I didn't want to be a teacher. I remember myself saying, "I don't want to be a regular school teacher, but I want to work with people." I got an undergraduate degree in recreation and park administration. It was interesting and fun, and I enjoyed working with people.

Then I just fell into a master's program in early childhood special education. That sounded cool. I could play, I had the adult component because I had the parent part, I had the child component, and I wasn't a regular teacher. Then we moved out here. To get certified I would have had to go back to school because my undergraduate degree wasn't in education.

Through our first experience in a childbirth class, that's really how I jumped into childbirth education. I said well, that would be a neat thing to do. I have a young child, I can stay at home with my children, and work with parents and stay sort of a teacher, and I'm working with people. So I went through that program. Then just as I looked to reenter [the work force] after our third child, it sort of flowed into parent education.

Suzanne Cardiff

I don't think I really chose it. I grew up caring for kids since I was 12. I started out babysitting. While I was going to college, I was working at a day care center as the assistant teacher. My mom's in social work (she's been doing it for 10 years this July), and she's got her master's, so I've got a lot of influence from her. She worked for child protective services back home, and they had an opening for temporary work—better pay than I was getting at day care, so I went for it. I thought it would be something good. The job was like what I have now. You get to show parents what to do with their kids and make sure they're doing appropriate things. I like doing that because it helps the kids. So that's how I got into it. I tried it and liked it.

Heidi Daly

I always wanted to be a social worker in a hospital, but I realized it is 10 times more difficult than working in a nursing home. You lose a lot of people working in a nursing home. You're around death a lot and the possibility of death, but the acute care, I don't think I could have dealt with that as well as the long-term care. There is so much more tragedy, and I don't think I could have effectively helped people. I probably would have been crying right along with them. In the hospitals they're young, they're babies, they're teenagers, they're my sister's age with babies, and I don't think I could've walked away at night and put it aside.

I chose to be a social worker because I liked working with people. I liked the feeling of helping somebody and the rewards I got from that, the touch, the hand on your hand, the look of gratitude and relief in their eyes, the tears and things like that when something worked out really well. As I went on in social work at a nursing home, it was frequent that that happened. It was very easy to get those rewards because of the giving part—people in nursing homes, they don't get a lot of that. They don't get a lot of somebody doing something for them. It was very fulfilling.

Jennifer Echarte

I began my work in human services because I've always had a desire—no, a talent—with people who couldn't speak up for themselves, people who didn't know what to ask for. I have seen so much in my life, between drug abuse and physical and sexual abuse and eating disorders. I've just seen so many different problems. I've faced so many different aspects of human nature that are usually considered negative. I've been around people in my personal life who have been able somehow to rationalize themselves losing control. In many ways, I'm young and naive, and there's so much that I don't know, but my childhood prepared me for facing that loss of control.

William Esp

Well, actually I think it was pretty serendipitous. For one, I'm a recovering alcoholic and addict, and when I went into my recovery I was making my living as a musician. I just kind of wandered around for a few years, and eventually a pre-med student in a restaurant that I was working at literally drug me to Metro [Metropolitan State College]. At the time I was 29 and had barely graduated from high school. I was going to be a rock star, so I did what I could to get through high school. I had very, very minimal confidence in myself academically.

So I went to Metro and just took general courses. I knew I was into social sciences, I remember that, so I took Intro to Sociology, Intro to Human Services, and an English course and just fell in love with school. At that point, I'd been sober about 2 1/2 years, and I met a human services instructor, Brenda Watson. She actually died before I finished Metro, but she had a profound influence on me—her and Dr. Dave Weiland. Of psychology, sociology, and human services, I liked human services.

Pamela Meister

I'd been in sales for so many years, and I enjoyed the challenge of persuasion. I sold medical equipment, I sold yellow pages advertising, I sold health care programs, insurance programs. It was wonderful, and I did it awfully hard. I did it with high integrity. However, after I was able to convince someone to purchase, that kind of left me feeling very empty. I listened to a Deepak Chopra tape, and he talked about how if you do something you feel in your heart, then you will be successful, and the success will be coming from what you feel.

I had checked into being a patient representative when I had lived in Chicago. It was just a volunteer type program. I came out here and checked again. It was still volunteer, and I couldn't afford that. Then when I got laid off [from sales], I was just going to do what felt right, not going to worry about money, and this was open.

They had six other people, and they actually told me in my initial interview with human resources that they had people who applied from within, and I probably didn't have a great chance, but they would put my application in anyway. I said, "Please do," and they hired me. So, I was shocked and thrilled and felt like it was supposed to be.

Christa Pavlus

I am a very people-oriented person. At first I thought I wanted to do architecture or something like that, but it was very boring. There were no people. I hated sitting with no people around me. All it took was a drafting class to learn that I hated that.

Then I decided I really wanted to work with abused children. And then I decided I could not handle that. I remember watching this thing about the rhesus monkeys that they used, about neglected monkeys. I was upset for a week, and I thought I would be a very miserable person [working with] children.

So, I decided to go into occupational therapy. When I first heard [about] occupational therapy, I didn't realize what all was involved in it and how many different aspects there were. I started out thinking I wanted to work in business, teaching body mechanics and proper workstations and things like that, but as I started doing my affiliations, I just really started falling in love with people.

Cathy Phelps

I think human services picked me, particularly victim assistance. I got involved in it totally by accident. I was taking a college class entitled Modes of Oppression. I always thought about oppression being related to ethnicity, but when we started talking about it relating to gender, some speakers came in from the local rape crisis center. I thought, "Oh my God, women, gender, oppression, how it all connects," with sexual violence being the epitome of how you control a class of people, and then that being layered with and complicated with issues of race. Being African American, I just thought, "Oh my God, this is it." I've always been interested in how people stay healthy and understanding how sexual violence affects that, how ethnicity affects that all sort of came together for me. It really chose me.

Then my roommate and I signed up to go through the rape crisis center training. I was the only woman of color in the group, and it was just an incredible training experience. But after training, when we went to sign up for our shift at the rape crisis center, I said, "Oh I can't do this, I can't do this now. I'm sorry, I've made a mistake." I literally backed out of the room where people were signing up and went home. A couple of weeks later, a woman called. She said, "Hey Cathy, I'm calling to schedule for next month's rape crisis center shifts," and before I could say, "Oh no, I'm not really sure about this," I'd signed up for a shift. I took my first shift, had my first crisis call from a rape victim, and I was on my way.

Johnn Young

I chose human services work because I felt like I needed to make a difference in the world, helping people be in a better place than where they were when they first started talking to me. To see that light go on inside that they've got it and that they realize there's something that they can do to change their lives always made me feel better. So, I guess I chose human services work because I get so much out of it. Even when there's bad days, I feel like, okay, today is not a good day, but tomorrow will be better. Somebody tomorrow will get it. Somebody will understand that what's going on with them right now is only temporary, and somewhere, somehow, even if they don't tell me directly, hopefully there'll be a change.

Mary Anne Harvey and Cheryl Lammers were interviewed at length for both the first and second editions. Their stories appear in Chapter 9. These excerpts from their interviews discuss why they chose human services careers.

Mary Anne Harvey

Some human services agencies were managed badly and had many problems, . . . and people did not bring good business practices and principles to the human services field. I thought that was outrageous. Bad management caused a tremendous waste of money and people's time and was unfair to the people who didn't get good services. So, I decided if I was going to stay in human services, I would end up in administration.

Cheryl Lammers

My rewards and satisfaction come from smaller-scale accomplishments, such as getting one client plugged into a complete program of services that enables him to feel happier and more comfortable with the world around him. Similarly, I feel satisfaction when a client feels more in control of his or her life and future path. . . . In some cases, I want the clients to know that there is someone who cares and will be honest and consistent in dealings with them.

ACKNOWLEDGMENTS

For the second edition, thanks to the anonymous reviewers of the second edition proposal for their helpful content suggestions. Thanks also to Dr. Ed Zuckerman for permission to adapt his forms for use with interviewees.

For the first edition, thanks to Becky Albracht, David Calderwood, Roger Freeby, Dr. Therese Hustis, Sara Johnson, and Guinn Rogers for working through and commenting on a draft of the entire manuscript as I wrote it.

Thanks to Nina Cruchon and Sally Mather for reading, commentary, and support throughout the writing of the first edition; to Dr. Andy Sweet and Dr. Jon Ziarnik, who read and commented on the last draft of the manuscript and helped shape the final version; to Jeff Slemons, whose art for the first edition captured the spirit of the book; and to Judith Halaszyn, co-author of the first edition, who created Disillusioned Diana and her friends.

Thanks to John Leslie, Karen Litz, and Dr. Jon Ziarnik for specific content ideas; to Randy Chapman for several vignettes related to legal issues; to Mary Ervolina for several vignettes related to social work; and to students in human services classes at Metropolitan State College for telling why they want to work in human services and for many conversations during guest lectures for them.

Thanks also to Brenda Watson and Dr. Bob Watson for their invitations to come into their classes, to Brenda Watson for her comments on the manuscript, and to the many people currently working in human services who were willing to tell why they do it and to share stories about their work.

An author couldn't ask for better treatment than I get from Brookes Publishing, especially from Melissa Behm, who has been my editor four times, including both editions of this book. By the time this second edition sees the light of day, my relationship with them will be more than 20 years old. My grateful thanks, especially for their patience with the initial fits and starts of the new edition.

Finally, my thanks to Cami Learned and Dr. Megan Miller, two outstanding human services professionals, for reading and commenting on both editions; for moral and practical support; and, most important, for being the kind of friends who last a lifetime.

Again, in memory of my father
Allen L. Bernstein, Ed.D.
He would have liked this book.

"Human services?
. . . That must be so rewarding."

SECTION I

Human Services Professional

CHAPTER 1

On Knowing Yourself
or

What's a Nice Person Like You Doing in a Job Like This?

OBJECTIVES

- Identify your reasons for selecting a human services career.

- Describe the strengths that you bring to your work.

- Describe personal characteristics that may limit your professional performance.

- Describe typical constraints on your performance that are created by external problems.

THE TALE OF DISILLUSIONED DIANA

One year after college graduation, four former classmates gather at Joe's Club to compare notes on their new careers and professions. In the group are an accountant; a paralegal; a computer systems analyst; and Diana, a probation officer. There is talk of opportunities to advance within organizations and comparisons of office sizes and amenities. The bragging moves on to who has the most perks, who has the best cell phone, who has the fastest computer, who has the classiest car, and who has rubbed elbows with the movers and shakers. As the bravado gradually diminishes, someone turns to Diana and asks her about her work. Diana tries to evade the attention with trite phrases such as "I enjoy the challenge," "It's very demanding dealing with people," and "It gives me a sense of fulfillment."

Later, back in her downtown efficiency apartment, Diana lets the frustration from the reunion flood over her. She feels cheated and disillusioned. She has no perks and no amenities, mountains of paperwork, no easy answers, and problems bigger than she ever imagined. Diana wants a way out. She picks up the evening paper and begins to circle want ads while muttering to herself, "No one ever warned me what human services would really be like."

Then the mail carrier delivers a package. Diana starts to open the box and thinks, "Oh—it's the book I ordered last month. It's probably too late to be useful now, but I don't have anything better to do." She opens to page one of *"Human services? . . . That must be so rewarding": A Practical Guide to Professional Development, Second Edition.*

KNOWING YOUR PROFESSIONAL MOTIVATION

People who choose to work in the human services have chosen to serve other people, to "do good." Therefore, the obvious answer to the question of why you have selected human services work is something like "to help people." Having said that, you have identified your motives for doing human services work, right?

Well, not exactly. It is important to be more specific about your motives for engaging in a particular type of work, to identify what makes you want to come to work every day and what rewards you get out of your work. If the work you do does not meet your professional needs, it is not likely that you will be able to do a good job of meeting other people's needs. Most of us need to do work that makes us feel good about ourselves, work that we see as valuable. This is especially necessary for human services professionals because we often get mixed messages from both our colleagues and the world at large about the worth of what we do.

THE "I'M JUST A . . ." PROBLEM

If we do not value what we do, we may suffer from the "I'm just a . . ." problem. This problem of thinking that your job is not very valuable is most obvious at parties when people ask, "What do you do?" and you answer, "Oh, I'm just a social worker," or, "I just do direct care." Sometimes the words "I'm just a . . ." are not spoken, but your tone of voice says the same thing, usually by sounding apologetic. People who describe their work by saying "I'm just a . . ." or by sounding apologetic are saying that what they do is not really valuable in their own eyes or in the eyes of other people. Our society may foster this attitude, but it is not healthy for you or your clients. If you are going to work in human services, you need to know what makes your work valuable to you, to the people you serve, and to society as a whole.

DEFINING MOTIVES: "THAT MUST BE SO REWARDING"

Let's go back to the party where, when asked what you do, you identified yourself as a human services professional. If you have been chatting with someone who is not in human services, chances are that this person's response will be something like "That must be very challenging work"; "I wish I could do that, but there's not enough money in it"; "Oh, you must have so much patience"; or, most often, "That must be so rewarding." These comments really mean "I don't understand what you get out of doing that stuff, but I guess it's good someone wants to do it." Similarly, family members and close friends may react with critical comments such as "Why don't you want to work with normal people?" or "How are you going to support yourself on such a small salary?"

DEFINING MOTIVES: SOME VIEWS
FROM HUMAN SERVICES PROFESSIONALS

It is true that people in human services typically receive fewer tangible (especially financial) rewards than people working in business as well as less status and recognition than people working in the for-profit world. Those who find human services work satisfying are able to identify the nonmonetary rewards they get from their work, such as seeing a small but significant change in someone's life or being thanked by someone who has used their services.

Ellen Berlin

People laugh at me at work, but it never feels like work.
You get paid for it—you get reimbursed because that's of course

our system—but it doesn't feel like work because I love it, and it's exciting. I'm just passionate about teaching. It's such a wonderful thing to support people in looking at pieces of themselves. So, I love that we all have a wonderful journey in this world and we all can make that journey for ourselves. I love talking about that, facilitating that, and philosophizing about that.

Suzanne Cardiff

I like the kids mostly. I like when the parents can change. That makes you feel good about yourself 'cause you know you're helping the kids. When the kids feel safer around you than around their parents, I like that, not 'cause I don't want them to feel safe around their parents but I want them to feel somebody's safe. Usually we get kids and they've been having such a hard life that they don't feel safe around anybody. They don't trust anybody. I like changing their attitudes.

Heidi Daly

I liked the working with the people, not only the patients but the family members, the staff, working as a team, working with other places in the community, and seeing how everything kind of clicked together, how everybody came together and solved the problems. That was something I really enjoyed doing, and I felt that I was good at coordinating.

Jennifer Echarte

Every day of my job is different. Every client, every time I see them it's a different experience. I'm on the road all the time, so I'm in homes, and I'm not an authority. I'm now working with adolescents. I'm not a teacher; I'm not anybody who's there to challenge them. I'm there to help them, so it's always a rewarding experience for me. I really feel that I want to give back a little. I feel like I've been really lucky in my life, and there are many people who aren't. So, the rewarding part of it is maybe giving some hope to people. I've always just enjoyed my work because I'm helping.

William Esp

To really be effective in this field you have to work on yourself constantly, on your own growth and development. I've really liked being able to learn more about myself almost on a daily basis. The other thing that I love about the work, I think particularly with addictions, is bringing that spiritual element. The spiritual elements of my life are actually a part of my work, which I don't think too many people get to do. When I say "spiritual" I mean that in the broadest context. I don't necessarily mean a belief in God or getting people to believe in God. I think of it in terms of synchronistic events, the things that create connection, the things that create a sense of wholeness for people.

In doing addictions work, it's working at what the addiction is about metaphorically for the person. Initially so many people come in, and they feel like there's no meaning in what's happened to them. I connect their experience to mine, to some aspects of my own recovery as well as all the recovery I've witnessed as a member of 12-step programs and working with other individuals.

Pamela Meister

I feel like I can make a positive impact in someone's life. [When] people come in [to the hospital], they're usually in a crisis situation in some way, shape, or form, and it's very intimidating. The system itself is intimidating, and then you complicate that with their particular illness or their loved one's illness. Just for me to be able to say, "Relax, you don't need to be worried about that, let me get you through this, and you concentrate on that," to see I made a difference, to see it on their faces, that's tremendously rewarding to me.

Christa Pavlus

I have always been a very people-oriented person, but I've always been a prissy little thing. I didn't ever want to get my hands dirty or anything like that, but the more I did I was so drawn to it. I loved the idea of working with people day in and day out. I need to be with people. I'm a talker and kind of an emotional person. I just have a bond with people, and I like to be with them.

Cathy Phelps

I feel like I can make a difference. I like seeing the resiliency of human beings. I like being able to talk about political issues, social issues, and how they interrelate. I like being able to use literature that way (my undergrad was in English, psychology, anthropology, and a little bit of women's studies). Then when I got my graduate degree, I realized that psychology wasn't enough. I didn't see me, my experience. So, I chose to get my master's degree in medical anthropology because I felt like that could really address the kinds of things, intervention and therapy-wise, that I wanted to address with women. Medical anthropology essentially is public health with culture thrown in, so it's the ability to use who you are, what your experience is, and your worldview to come up with new strategies.

You can make a difference, and you can use this difference to help people make transitions in their lives. I like being able to educate people about history and culture and why someone's approach to an experience might be different than what the textbook says it should be. [I like] having a role as a social change agent, making a life of what I give and get.

Johnn Young

When it works it's rewarding, and it's the kind of work where there's always something to do. My partner will say to me, "Well, are you done yet?" and I always tell him I don't leave when I'm done, I leave when my hours are up or I'm tired. If I stayed until I was done, I would never go home. So, the good part is I know that there's always going to be something to do. It's a gold mine of potential out there, and once you've hit that mother lode, as they used to call it, there's always a nugget or a diamond to pull out, and there's always going to be something to do.

Exercises

1-1. Ask several human services professionals or human services students whom you know why they do human services work and why they *chose* to do human services work (the two may not be the same).

1-2. Write down the comments you have received from family and friends who do not understand your reasons for choosing human services work.

THE TALE OF DISILLUSIONED DIANA, CONTINUED

Diana reads the first section of the book, comes to the exercises, picks up a pencil, and begins writing answers as she says to herself, "It can't hurt, and just maybe it will help me figure out what to do next. I really do enjoy my job when I get a kid back in school and off the streets. It's also true that I dread the long court hearings and distraught parents when all too often the kids get deeper into trouble with the law.

"Mom would be delighted if I changed careers—became 'respectable' and stopped working with the 'dregs' as she calls them. Every time she says that, I get so angry. . . .

"Tomorrow I'll try to talk with Rudy. . . . He's been a probation officer for 10 years and still cares. I'll ask him how he keeps going."

IDENTIFYING YOUR OWN MOTIVES

It is important for you to know your motives for entering or continuing human services work. If you are not sure why you are doing the work you do, it will be difficult to deal with the mixed social messages you will receive about the worth of human services work.

This section consists mostly of exercises designed to help you identify your motives for working in human services. Before starting the exercises, however, consider the difference between being selfish and being self-caring. When we refer to an action as selfish and regard it negatively, we usually mean that the person doing it is not taking others into account. That does *not* mean, however, that all self-caring behavior is selfish. It is important to consider both your needs and those of the people you serve. As you complete the exercises, remember the following rules of thumb:

1. It is okay to have self-caring motives as well as motives based on caring for others. For instance, one of the author's motives for writing this book is to satisfy a desire to help human services professionals. Another motive is to make some money from the sales of the book.
2. It is okay to have fun while you work. It is possible to do serious work and have a good time doing it. Do not assume there is something wrong with having fun at work.
3. It is also okay to have unselfish motives such as making people's lives a little easier.
4. It is *not* okay to do human services work because you think you should find it rewarding or because you believe people will think you are a good person. Whatever you do, do it because *you* want to, not because someone else wants you to. People who genuinely like their work and find it rewarding usually do better work than people who do not like what they do.

Exercises

1-3. If you are still in training, you may not be familiar with what people in your profession do on a day-to-day basis. There are several ways to find out. Do one of the following:

   a. Interview one or more people who are currently doing the type of work you plan to do. Ask them to describe what they do in the course of a typical day. Also, ask them to identify the tasks they find most satisfying and those they find least satisfying.

   b. By signing up for internships and/or volunteer work, expose yourself to a variety of experiences in the types of organizations and professions you are considering.

   c. Arrange to shadow someone in your profession for a day, noting the different things that she or he does. If you do not know anyone to ask, call a human services agency, and explain who you are and why you want to shadow someone. Anticipate the fact that the person you shadow needs to get approval from a supervisor and may have trouble finding time in his or her schedule to fit you in.

   During all of these exercises, be sure to note not only core activities such as counseling but also support activities such as paperwork and driving. Also pay attention to the environments in which the work is done. For example, how much privacy is there? How much noise?

1-4. Using your experience or the information you collected while doing Exercise 1-3, write a description of a typical work day for the type of job that interests you. Following is an example for a caseworker in a small social services office:

   8:00   Report in; check voice mail for messages; return telephone calls from people seeking benefits.

   9:00   Conduct meetings with potential benefits recipients; complete multiple forms for each person.

   11:00   Compile memos to files for people seen today; send paperwork and recommendations to supervisor.

   12:00   Lunch

   12:30   Attend department meeting.

   1:30   Investigate possible child abuse situation; make on-site assessment (includes 45 minutes travel round trip).

   3:30   Meet with department attorney to discuss findings.

   4:00   Finish memos to files.

4:30   Make list of things to do for tomorrow.
4:45   Leave; get stuck in rush-hour traffic.
5:30   Arrive home—hot, fussy, and frustrated.

1-5.   Using all the information you have gathered about your chosen career, answer the following questions:
   a.   What are you or will you be required to do that you like to do?
   b.   Of the activities that you like to do, which activities do you like the most? Why?
   c.   What are you or will you be required to do that you do not like to do?
   d.   Of the activities that you do not like to do, which are you most likely to avoid? Why?

Suzanne Cardiff

I don't like working with parents who don't care and don't want their kids or who give you this speech about who are you to tell me how to take care of my kids. It's kind of like running yourself into a wall. Also, I have a hard problem when you think you're on a road to helping a parent, and maybe your supervisors or the agency think that's not the way you should be doing it or that it's not your job to be doing it even if you're the only one who's making any progress. That is a huge problem, I think, for everybody. You have to follow so many rules.

Heidi Daly

There's a lot of paperwork and a lot of bureaucracy. You don't get the time that you want with the patients. That's part of the reason I left the first time and this time. It was just pulling me away from the patients. I didn't see an end to it. I didn't feel I was helping the patients as well as I could have been. The first time I was at a nursing home, I was there for about 2½ years. It was very stressful. I was the only social worker for 110 residents. At the time there were a lot of changes in the state regulations, so a lot more responsibility was placed on me. There was more paperwork, there was more charting, there were more things that had to be done for the residents that fell back on me. It just got to the point where one social worker couldn't do it all. I requested a part-time helper and was denied by my administrator. It was like beating my head against the wall, and I just couldn't do it anymore.

Jennifer Echarte

What I dislike about it is probably the funding aspect of it. I think that so many people would prefer that people who are different and people who have problems and people who are sick aren't around. They're trying to pass a law that will make state taxes go up so that they can have a new stadium. Our clients have so little funding, and the mental health center is going to cut back a lot of jobs and go to shorter treatment. A lot of people are going to be cut off, and they're going to be wandering the streets. Public support for people who don't have it as well as other people do, it's just not there. United Way isn't getting the funding it used to, and Medicaid cannot provide the money they used to. There isn't so much support.

William Esp

The current climate, what's happened with managed care, it's really hard. The idea of somebody else dictating what care for my clients should be is appalling. There's just something fundamentally wrong with that. You try to give people all that you can give them and have just this short period of time, and yet you know with addictions, there's so many phases. You can tell them [managed care people] but they're not going to understand until they're there. So just that business end of it I really dislike.

Pamela Meister

I dislike the changes in the entire health care industry with cutbacks in health care for medically indigent [people who have no health insurance]. The system is set up to make it really difficult. In some cases I can see why, because some people have become very dependent on the system and don't look for other options. On the other hand, there are some people who don't have other options. It's really hard to sit and tell someone I can't do anything. That's the hardest thing.

Cathy Phelps

What I don't like is how quickly we in this discipline get stagnant and that sometimes I hear the same theory over and over again. Isn't anybody reading anything? Some of my peers and colleagues after they graduate and get their degrees they stop belonging to professional associations, they stop reading their journals, they stop trying to apply [their knowledge]. That's the part that's frustrating to me, the knowledge that so much of it is just talk and the knowledge of what I think can make a difference isn't being done. We still discuss domestic violence the way we've done it since I remember reading about domestic violence, and I think we should try different things. Also, I don't see any agency progress, after I give my time and energy. So that's real disappointing to me.

Johnn Young

What I dislike [and also like] about it is that there's always something to do. With my work and with the program, if I take a day off or if I take a week or 2 off, there isn't somebody to slide in and take my place. It's on hold until I come back, so that's what I dislike about it. I also dislike the fact that sometimes, being an African American, I'll be asked to do something that has nothing to do with what I'm capable of doing. It's just that somebody has decided I can do it. I've gotten to the point where I'll give a reference.

KNOWING YOUR STRENGTHS AND LIMITS

Most of us want to do good work, and if we are in human services, we want to be helpful. Part of doing good work is figuring out what you do well and where you need to improve your performance—in other words, identifying your strengths and limitations.

Strengths

We all bring a unique combination of strengths to our work. Some of them are professional, such as being good at teaching new skills to our clients or being familiar with many community resources. Some strengths are more general, such as the ability to get along with a group of diverse people or the ability to be a good friend. One of the advantages of working in human services is that the work frequently involves joining forces with other professionals whose strengths are different from and complementary to our own.

Knowing Your Limits

Identifying limitations that interfere with your performance is not the most appealing of pastimes. It is important, however, to know your limits because no one is perfect, and no one has all the answers. Although in the future you may have some of the answers that you do not have now, you will also have other questions that have not occurred to you yet. In the long run, you will be more effective if you assume the following:

1. I do not have all of the answers and probably do not even know all of the important questions.
2. Therefore, sometimes I am going to make mistakes, sometimes I won't know what to do, and sometimes I won't be able to overcome obstacles to getting work done.
3. It is okay to make mistakes, to not know what to do, or to encounter obstacles.
4. It is *not* okay to ignore my limitations.
5. It is not only okay but also desirable to ask for help or to try to change in order to do better work.

Personal Limits

Each of us has a different, unique combination of strengths and limitations. People in human services, however, often encounter some common problems.

You Do Not Like Everyone You Are Supposed to Serve   This is a tough lesson to learn, particularly when you have just started working in human services. There are, however, few saints among us. It is perfectly normal (if not always nice) to have personal likes and dislikes. So, most of us have to learn that we like some of the people we serve more than others and that we also like some of our colleagues more than others. This is acceptable, as long as you know how you feel and behave professionally toward everyone, not just those whom you like. It is not only possible, but necessary, to treat your colleagues and the consumers of your services with respect and courtesy, regardless of how you feel about them.

Furthermore, not all the people you serve will like you. Some will resent what you seem to represent (e.g., privilege, government control), others will resent needing help from anyone, and some will resent your professional expertise. Behaving professionally, even toward those who do not like you, is a necessity in human services work (see Chapters 2 and 4).

You Will Not Be Able to Save Everyone   You are not going to achieve the outcome you prefer with everyone you serve. Sometimes this occurs because you need better skills. For instance, if your work with foster families results in an encounter with someone who has a drinking problem, then you may not know how to help. A second reason you may not achieve the desired outcome is that some people do not want to be helped in the way you want to help them. For example, you may be trying to help a family keep a child with severe mental health problems at home, but the family may want you to find an out-of-home placement. A third reason is that sometimes people do not want the same outcomes you want for them. For example, a couple may want to save their marriage even though you believe that doing so is unhealthy for both of them. A fourth reason is that sometimes you simply do not have enough control over the situation to achieve the desired outcome. For example, some people shop around until they find professionals who will tell them exactly what they want to hear. Human services professionals often encounter these sorts of obstacles.

There Is Never Enough Time   Not having enough time is related to the problem of not being able to save everyone. There is always more to do and more people who might be served than there is time to serve them. Human services professionals who do not learn to live with this lesson generally burn out rather quickly. You have to learn to manage professional time (see Chapter 5) and to take time to meet your personal needs (see Chapter 8). Most of us have relationships (e.g., with friends and family) and activities (e.g., recreation, hobbies, community service) that are important to us and are not work related. When we fail to meet our personal needs, our professional performance usually suffers.

There Will Always Be Things About Your Work and the People with Whom You Work that Cause Strong Emotional Reactions   In certain situations, something "pushes your buttons." You do not react rationally, even though you know you are overreacting. The triggering factor may be a certain tone of voice, a specific type of problem, or a form to fill out. All of us have hot buttons. The first step toward coping with things that set you off is to figure out what they are. For instance, a colleague's voice may sound just enough like your older sister that you react to her as though she were your sister instead of a peer.

You May Not Want to Do Human Services Work for the Rest of Your Life   The average life span keeps increasing, and many people have more than one career during their lives—human services professionals are no exception. One common reason for a career change is development of new interests, either in a different aspect of human services or in something altogether different. Another common reason for a career change is that you no longer find your work rewarding enough. There is nothing wrong with this. Seldom do we find all the same things rewarding throughout our lives.

William Esp

When you look at these challenges, you're talking about making that transition from school to work. School is an ideal environment. I love school and theory, but then you get out there, and you have business, and you have managed care. You have these ideas of what the perfect caseload is, and you'll find out that it's about twice that. Everybody has to do twice as much as what the ideal is, and you have to take care of yourself, which sometimes means doing a little less than you might do just because the overall cost in the big picture of things is just way too great.

External Limits

In addition to the personal limitations described previously, human services workers encounter other constraints. These external limits are inherent in the structure of our systems for delivering human services.

There Is Not Enough Money   There are two main financial limitations in human services, underfunded entitlement programs and non-entitlement programs that can't afford to serve all those who are eligible. By law, entitlement programs must serve everyone who meets the basic eligibility criteria for them. Public schools, for example, are entitlement programs: They must serve all school-age children. When entitlement programs do not have enough money, everyone is served, but they are not served as well as they would be with additional resources. When a human services program is not an entitlement program, usually there is not enough money to serve all eligible people.

Some Programs Work Against Social Values Instead of Promoting Them   The care and protection of children is supposed to be highly valued by most cultures. Since the 1990s the welfare system in the United States has been undergoing major revisions intended to get more people off of welfare and into the work force, including single parents with young children. It is unclear, however, whether there is enough child care available for those children and whether former welfare recipients can earn enough to pay for it. There is a possibility that getting people back to work will endanger their children. Human services professionals who work with people affected by welfare reform may be faced with changing responsibilities and may be told to implement policy changes with which they disagree.

No One Knows Everything   There are some human problems that we do not know enough about to solve completely. Human services professionals do not have the knowledge, for example, to cure all child molesters or to end all domestic violence.

Changing External Limits   External, systemic limits such as these can ultimately be overcome only by people with the power and knowledge to change our systems. If you want to devote yourself to changing systemic limits in human services, you will need to become an advocate, an administrator, a policy maker, or a researcher.

Exercises

1-6.   List all of the strengths you bring to your work. If you are not sure what they are, ask colleagues, classmates, supervisors, or teachers for help with identifying them.

1-7.   List all of the personal limits that have the potential to interfere with your professional performance. Pick the three that could cause the most interference. Some examples follow:
- Unreliable car, job requires lots of local travel
- New in town, not familiar with local resources
- Father was an alcoholic, anger at him will probably interfere with ability to help other substance abusers; impatient with people who are not helping themselves

1-8.   Which of your personal strengths compensate for the limits you listed above? Some examples follow:
- Thoroughly familiar with public transportation
- Good at doing practical research, finding out about local resources
- Have been a recipient of social services, know how it feels, care about/interested in people

1-9.   List all of the external limits that are likely to interfere with your professional performance. Pick the three that are most serious in relation to your current or anticipated responsibilities. Some common examples include the following:
- Overcrowded office space
- Waiting lists for services
- Unrealistic deadlines
- Noisy work areas
- Limited funding
- Government regulations

1-10.   Of the limits you listed in answer to Exercise 1-9, which are most likely to bother you? Why? You may find it useful to discuss these exercises with your classmates or colleagues. (You are not the only one who experiences these limits!)

Which Way Do the Scales Tip?

No matter what type of work you choose to do, it will have some advantages and some disadvantages. In most jobs, some of what you do will give you the professional rewards you desire, and some of what you do will be unpleasant to you. Each of us is unique in terms of what we find rewarding and what we find unpleasant. Furthermore, each of us is different in our judgment of which unpleasant activities we are willing to perform in order to do what we find professionally rewarding. Each of us needs a different level of professional reward to keep doing what we do.

It is not enough, however, to know what your professional rewards and costs are. You also need to know what sort of balance you require between positives and negatives for the end result to be positive. Most of us can tell whether we are happy with our work. When we are happy with our work, we like going to work in the morning, and we feel proud of what we do. When we are not happy with our work, we usually do not jump out of bed bright-eyed and bushy-tailed. (Of course, some of us never jump out of bed bright-eyed and bushy-tailed, but that's a different problem.)

The difficulty is not figuring out whether you are happy with your work. Instead, the difficulty lies with identifying the specific factors that make the difference between being happy professionally and wanting to find a different job or even a different profession. People can be dissatisfied with their work for any one of a number of reasons. They may be spending too much time doing things they find unpleasant. They may be doing too few of the things they find rewarding. Or, the problem may be both too few rewards and too many undesirable activities.

To complicate matters even further, sometimes people working in human services are dissatisfied not because they dislike their work but because of the effects their work has on their personal lives. Most human services professionals cannot help spending some of their time away from work thinking about and often worrying about the people they serve. *When you work in human services, you can't punch out!* We take worries about the people we serve home with us and usually find it very difficult to simply shut a file drawer and forget them at 5:00 P.M. When your work takes too much of your attention during the rest of your life, however, you may find yourself dissatisfied with that work. It may have a negative effect on your personal life, particularly your personal relationships. That is why it is important to find a healthy balance between the professional and the personal. Chapters 5 and 8 discuss ways to manage time and stress so that this is possible.

Exercise

1-11.   Do the advantages of your chosen work outweigh the disadvantages? If not, you may want to look into ways to change that balance, such as career development (see Chapter 7) or stress management (see Chapter 8). You may want to repeat this exercise every 3–6 months.

THE TALE OF DISILLUSIONED DIANA CONTINUES

Two weeks later, Diana thinks, "Finally, a quiet evening, no home visits to do, nothing good on the tube. Maybe I'll work on those exercises again. It sure helped to talk with Rudy. In fact, I've been feeling more positive about my job lately. I guess mostly I worry that I'm not skilled enough to solve the problems my clients have, and I'm afraid I'll let them down. "Well, let's see what my answers to Exercise 1-11 look like."

Disadvantages
High recidivism rate with juvenile offenders
Red tape and more red tape
Office in a dangerous part of town
No respect from family and some of my friends
Clients and families resent what I stand for: courts, criminal records, sign
*   of failure.*

Advantages
Experiencing the satisfaction of seeing a kid "make it"
Having a family and a client say thanks
My supervisor encourages me to attend seminars and workshops to
*   improve my skills.*
Co-worker support
My hours are very flexible.
I have the authority to make decisions and am responsible for them.

"Hmm—it's about even. Somehow, putting it on paper makes it real. I think I'll hang it on the wall by my desk as a reminder and add to both lists as I think of things."

CHAPTER 2

On Minding Other People's Business
or
Who Appointed You?

OBJECTIVES

- Acknowledge that the people receiving human services are people first and clients second.

- Recognize the rights of people who receive human services and the implications of those rights for service providers.

Cathy Phelps

When you're asking someone to do something, you think, "Would I do that, could I do that?" Questions that I hear myself asking a client or student and I realize I don't know the answers—I better find them.

Put yourself into the following story: Your next door neighbor, who has an answer to every problem from split ends to toxic waste, stops you as you leave for work in the morning. "I see you have leaves plugging up your gutters. Now, the way to fix that is. . . yadda, yadda, yadda. We have to keep up property values in the neighborhood. . . yadda, yadda, yadda." This is the last thing you want to hear at 7:30 A.M. as you leave for work. You feel yourself getting angrier by the minute, and as you get into your car, you mutter, "Who appointed you as my watchdog, anyway?"

PEOPLE FIRST

Everyone in human services works directly or indirectly to help people. A desire to help people is the reason most of us choose human services work. Unfortunately, we sometimes forget that people are the center of our efforts. When we focus on the problem instead of the person, we lose sight of our desire to help people, and we lose effectiveness. It is important to remember that the people we serve are people first and clients second.

One of the most serious mistakes that human services workers can make is to focus on only the problems and not the strengths of the people they are trying to serve. We tend to devalue people when we see only their problems, faults, and lack of skills. We are all imperfect, and we all have problems. Nonetheless, most of us manage to lead reasonably productive lives and make some contributions to the world. We are all entitled to respect and recognition for our contributions.

THE RIGHT TO BE TAKEN SERIOUSLY

When we see the people we serve as people, we treat them with respect. We remember we are there to provide them with a service, and we take them seriously.

Heidi Daly

The patient abuse, I just couldn't turn my head, and I couldn't fight my boss. It was like beating my head against a wall. I feel that nobody should have to put up with that abuse, so I left.

Jennifer Echarte

A lot of the people that I work with in the mental health center are ostracized. You know how children are kind of cruel to one another, you know how, in school, kids have a way of being really mean and nasty and doing horrible things? Well, I've had clients come to me and say, "I tried that job at McDonald's but I have never been so insulted in my life. I walked out crying because they were saying 'Are you weird? What's that twitch?' " People really have a hard time dealing with people who are different from them. I don't know why it is, if it's discomfort or not understanding. But their reaction a lot of times is to make fun and to put down. It makes them feel better somehow. I really don't understand that.

Cathy Phelps

It's a privilege to have somebody trust you with these intimate kinds of details of their life. Remember that when you're working with people, and remember that it really is a privilege to be in a room with them.

A Sad Story

The Helpful Home is a residence for six adults with developmental disabilities. The direct services staff are underpaid and have far too many responsibilities. The program director, Ian Torgerson, is giving a tour of the home to Dr. Vera Gardner. He says, as they walk in the door, "I'm sure you can appreciate the difficulty this facility presents for me from a supervision standpoint, as it's located several miles from my office. We try to deal with those problems by having very detailed procedures that the staff must follow." He walks her through the dining room, where staff are gathered, without introducing them. As the tour proceeds, staff are heard grumbling in the background.

Ian goes on, "Some of the residents have some fairly serious self-stimulatory behaviors; some of these behaviors are self-injurious." He goes to a resident and walks him over to Vera. "Sam, here, for example, often flaps his hands to self-stimulate." While he is talking, Sam starts to flap his hands. "Of course, we use all the latest treatment techniques to deal with this serious problem."

Ian and Vera go off to view the residents' bedrooms while Sam starts to flap more wildly and begins hitting himself.

Obviously the professionals in this story did not take Sam seriously. Whom in your life do *you* take seriously? Are the people whom you serve on this list? Here are some of the cues that society uses to tell us which people to take seriously:

- They carry briefcases.
- They wear three-piece suits.
- They have money.
- They have the keys.
- They have political power.

When we take people seriously, we

- Listen to their opinions and suggestions
- Ask for their input
- Address them in the same way we expect to be addressed
- Make eye contact when we talk with them
- Assume what they want may be different from what we want for them
- Interact with them in languages they understand
- Respect their physical space

When we do not take people seriously, we

- Do not give them our complete attention, often by writing or by talking on the telephone while they are with us
- Do not make eye contact with them
- Assume we have the answers for them
- Assume our answers are better than theirs
- Talk about them in front of others (often while they are standing there)
- Describe them in negative terms (e.g., "manipulative," "a problem")
- Do not ask for their input or suggestions
- Address them by their first names but expect them to call us Ms., Mr., or Dr.
- Invade their physical space without their permission
- Interrupt them or finish thoughts for them

> *The power of the expert is very great and the way in which an expert sees you may easily become the way in which you see yourself.*
>
> (Remen, 1996, p. 235)

Pamela Meister

Reaching some of the people that have a natural distrust of the system, overcoming that obstacle, is a communication challenge. What works is establishing a personal connection; really listening to what they're saying; getting past old history to where you can say okay, what do you need, and what can we do right now; just letting them know that I really am there for them; and building some kind of trust.

Perhaps you think lack of respectful behavior occurs infrequently in human services, but consider the rather sobering results of a recent study of elevator conversations in five different hospitals. Conversations that violated confidentiality, that raised concerns about the speaker's desire to provide high-quality care, that raised concerns about whether others were providing high-quality care, or that contained derogatory remarks about patients or their families occurred in 14% of the elevator rides observed (Ubel et al., 1995).

Ellen Berlin

Many parents, at some point along the course, they'll come and share that they're not treated in a way that anybody should be treated. We don't know whose truth is whose truth, and I know that, but even if it's a different truth, people don't need to be dealing with people in a way that disempowers them and demeans them and just keeps pushing them down.

The Need for Common Courtesy

Dr. Carolyn L. Vash provided one of the best descriptions of the ways in which human services professionals should act and sometimes do not. Dr. Vash is a psychologist who also has a physical disability. She has been both a provider and a consumer of human services. She reminds us that much of the difficulty in evaluation units comes from "failures of common courtesy and overconcern about one's own busy schedule at the expense of the clients' time" (1984, p. 256). Those sorts of problems are common to all human services, not just evaluation units. Dr. Vash continues:

> Most of our parents taught us better behavior, but somehow we forget. Rudeness sometimes begins the moment the client arrives. We do not introduce him to the other people present. We do not show him where to put his coat. We do not tell him where the restroom is. . . . We do not offer him a cup of coffee. . . . When shy people who fear the worst attend

social functions in our homes, we usually take the time and make special efforts to reassure and welcome them. When people who are scared to death visit our facilities, comparable efforts are in order. (1984, pp. 256–257)

It is important to take people seriously, especially the people you serve. If you show a lack of respect for them, then you are unlikely to gain their respect or trust, which significantly decreases your chances of being helpful to them.

It is also important to take yourself seriously and show self-respect. How can you expect others to have respect for the work you do if you do not?

Exercises

2-1. Describe at least two individuals you know who are taken seriously by others. How do people act around them?
2-2. Next, describe at least two individuals you know who are not taken seriously. How do people act around them?
2-3. What do you think are the most noticeable differences between the two groups of people you have described?
2-4. Describe in detail an experience you had in which you were not being taken seriously. What happened? How did you feel then?
2-5. Review the list of what we do when we take someone seriously (see p. 24). What would you add? List five more cues that you use to tell you whom to take seriously.
2-6. Repeat Exercise 2-5 for what we do when we do not take someone seriously (see p. 24).

ON CONFIDENTIALITY

Maintaining confidentiality is an important part of respecting the rights and dignity of those we serve. Most human services workers are privy to intimate information about people receiving services. Although the details of confidentiality laws and regulations vary from place to place and across different types of services, the fundamentals remain the same in most situations. We are required, whether ethically, legally, or both, to keep private information to ourselves unless there is a possibility of danger; in such cases, the law requires us to report the information. This means we should not talk about the people we serve by name or reveal other identifying information to individuals not involved directly in serving our clients.

William Esp

One of the things that was really, really critical for me to learn early on was the importance of basic stuff like getting releases of information to talk to anyone else that you're working with. Ethically it's just wrong not to do that, and I tell clients that when they come in. If they're seeing an individual therapist, I need to talk to this person because me telling the client one thing and that person telling the client another can do great harm.

Johnn Young

With what I do, having to talk to people about HIV and AIDS, there's a lot of times I hear horror stories. For the first year or 2 of doing this I'd go home, and I couldn't sleep because I heard horror stories about what people were doing. People would tell me that they'd go out, and they would do drugs, and then they would have sex with several different guys, and they wouldn't remember who the guys were. There was one particular story where a guy was having an affair, having unsafe sex with this person. They both were HIV positive, and he was sleeping with his partner who thought he was in a monogamous relationship. All I could do was try to convince him that this was not a good thing, to put someone he supposedly cared about in such danger. That was really, really difficult for me.

Well, how I came to terms with it: He felt comfortable enough to tell me the story. [I thought] okay, I can talk to him, I can try to find out what he's getting out of doing this, and maybe I can get him to see that this isn't the best way he could be. I figured he must trust me to tell me this. I've learned that I have to remember what my values are and that the biggest thing that I pride myself on is that if someone tells me something, it stays with me, that's it. I couldn't repeat it if I wanted to.

We cannot talk to any professional from another human services agency about an individual being served unless permission is obtained from the consumer, from that person's parent (if the consumer is a minor), or from the legal guardian. If the consumer is an adult and has not been declared incompetent, that person must agree before information is shared with anyone, including a spouse, parents, and other relatives. This does not mean professionals are prohibited from seeking consultation on how to improve what they do. When professionals discuss their work or seek consultation outside of their agencies, however, they are required to describe the situation without identifying the person involved. Johnn Young's previous description of a client, for example, omits identifying information.

The one standard exception to the rules on releasing confidential information is when people receiving services request that you release their records. Most of the time a signed written release is required that tells what information can be released to whom and within what time period. (Sometimes it is unclear whether an individual is competent to give consent. For a discussion of this issue, see Christensen, Haroun, Schneiderman, & Jeste, 1995; Gostin, 1995; Hulteng, 1991; Manning & Gaul, 1997; Morris, Niederbuhl, & Mahr, 1993; and Woody, 1984.)

Exercise

2-7. Determine which of the following is a breach of confidentiality:

a. A colleague from your agency who serves the same people as you calls and asks whether you know anything about an individual you are serving. You give him the information requested.

b. The father of a 22-year-old man receiving services from your organization calls to see how he is doing. You tell him.

c. A staff member from a nearby independent living center calls and asks for information about someone you served last month. You provide the information.

d. In the elevator on the way to your office, one of your colleagues says, "Hey, how's Sally Smith doing? I've heard she is making excellent progress." Your colleague also provides services to Sally Smith.

e. You go to lunch and leave a confidential file on your desk in your unlocked office.

f. You take a telephone call in a colleague's office, and it is about someone you serve.

Answers to Exercise 2–7

a. This is not a breach of confidentiality because you and your colleague both work for the same agency and provide services to the same person.

b. and c. These are definite breaches of confidentiality unless the father and the independent living center staff have obtained signed releases of information from the people receiving services.

d.   This is not a breach if no one else is in the elevator.

e.   This is a breach waiting to happen because the opportunity exists for an unauthorized person to read the file.

f.   This may or may not be a breach, depending on whether your colleague stays in the office, whether your colleague is also serving the person you discuss over the telephone, and whether you mention identifying information during the call.

ON USING AND ABUSING POWER

Human services workers are almost always in positions that give them power over the people they serve. Sometimes that power is overt, such as when a services provider has the power to decide whether an individual is eligible for a particular benefit. Sometimes the power is less obvious, such as when a professional has the power to help someone decide how to solve a personal problem. Even though many laws exist that protect the rights of people receiving services, service recipients may be too frightened, troubled, or unaware of their rights to exercise them.

Being in a position of power carries with it a special responsibility to refrain from abusing that power, especially with respect to sexual relationships. It is always unethical and usually illegal to engage in sexual relationships with anyone receiving services from you. In fact, the author considers a sexual relationship between any human services worker and a current consumer of services "professional rape." This may seem so obvious that it goes without saying, but the author has seen it happen in a variety of different situations. There is no excuse for engaging in a sexual relationship with someone you are serving as a human services professional. Some human services professionals who are confused and having personal problems of their own engage in sexual relationships with people they serve. This is unfortunate and unacceptable. Some human services professionals deliberately take sexual advantage of the people they are supposedly serving. This is also unacceptable and should be grounds for immediate termination and possible legal action.

Exercises

2-8.   Using your own experience and observations or those of other human services professionals in your field, identify five ways in which a human services professional could misuse power over a consumer of services.

2-9.   What are your ethical and legal obligations if you discover that one of your colleagues is engaging in a sexual relationship with a consumer of services?

FITTING THE SOLUTION TO THE PROBLEM

When all you have is a hammer, everything looks like a nail.
(Anonymous)

Most of us in human services are trained to use one particular type of approach to solving human problems. Counselors learn to counsel, therapists learn a particular type of therapy, and advocates learn to advocate and use legal solutions. It is natural to want to do what we are good at doing. That desire, however, can lead to a common mistake: defining problems in ways that allow us to pick our favorite solution for them. Following is a classic example.

Several years ago, the author was consulted about using a behavioral intervention to help a young woman with mental retardation to improve her communication skills. This seemed at first like a reasonable request. The people making the request were fairly skilled in teaching individuals similar to the young woman in question, and the author is an expert in behavioral interventions. The young woman's problem was that she almost always held her hand over her mouth while talking with people. During the discussion about this problem, the human services workers who made the referral were asked if the young woman in question was taking any medication (a standard question because many medications affect how people act). The staff reported she had been taking female hormone supplements ever since her ovaries had been removed because her body no longer produced any of those hormones itself. The hormone dosage, however, had not been reviewed by a physician for some time. Further discussion revealed that when the young woman held her hand over her mouth, she covered the mustache she had grown. Finally, a conversation with the young woman revealed she was quite embarrassed by her facial hair. The author refused to recommend a behavioral intervention. Instead, a medical evaluation of hormone levels was recommended because improper levels of hormones in women can lead to the growth of male secondary sex characteristics such as facial hair.

This situation is a classic example of two typical traps for people in human services. First, no one asked the person receiving help what she thought was the problem. Second, the people working with her tried to apply the solution they were good at applying instead of using the most effective solution for the problem.

The Least Intrusive Solution

> *When human beings are playing for stakes of happiness and self-knowledge, the only believable victories are probably the temporary and partial ones.*
>
> *(Mallon, 1984, p. 83)*

Identifying other people's problems is almost always easier than acknowledging our own mistakes. Designing solutions for others' problems is also much easier than coming up with solutions for our own shortcomings. This leads to the temptation to offer considerably more assistance than is wanted or needed. Here is an example.

A young woman who is 17 years old, has a minimum wage job, and is pregnant goes to a human services agency. She asks whether there are any classes she can attend that will teach her about nutrition for her child. The intake specialist suggests a class that is located an hour's bus ride away and costs $50. In addition, the specialist recommends enrollment in a vocational school so that the young woman can get a better job and assertiveness training because she appears to be rather shy. The young woman shakes her head and leaves. The specialist does not understand why the woman has left.

The specialist heads home at the end of the day, decides not to go work out because it is too much trouble, and proceeds directly to his lawyer's office. There, he discusses his divorce settlement.

How many of us have sparkling clean homes; beautiful yards; well-maintained cars; perfectly balanced budgets; completely nutritious diets; totally fulfilling personal relationships; and satisfying, successful careers? It is hardly fair to try to restructure someone else's life when your own is not in order. We cannot expect the people we serve to be more sane, more well-adjusted, more honest, or more independent than ourselves. Most of us cope as best we can with the trials and tribulations of being human, winning temporary victories and suffering occasional setbacks. People do have problems that can be solved with outside assistance; that is why human services exist. Not every problem, however, requires a human services intervention, nor does everyone with a problem want such assistance. Furthermore, most people who do accept our assistance want it to be as unintrusive as possible.

How can we determine whether the solutions we propose as human services professionals are as unintrusive as possible? Consider what makes a solution "intrusive." The more intrusive a solution is, the more it is

- Costly, in terms of time and/or money
- Difficult to use
- Disruptive to the person's privacy
- Incompatible with the client's personal values, cultural or ethnic practices, and/or religious beliefs

Thus, for each problem we try to solve, we should ask whether the solution we select is, of all possible solutions to the problem, the least costly, the least disruptive, the easiest to use, and the most compatible with client values.

Consider what the least intrusive solution might be for the situation cited previously, in which the 17-year-old woman was looking for nutrition training to prepare for her new baby. Perhaps the intake specialist could call the visiting nurses' office and arrange for the woman to call the office at her convenience to arrange a time for a visit to her home. Or, he could check to find out whether the community school nearest her home offers a useful course. Both these alternatives are relatively inexpensive, easy to use, and relatively easy to schedule.

> *Where should the authority of the caretaker leave off and*
> *the rights of the cared for begin?*
>
> *(Rothman, 1981a, p. xi)*

CONSUMER RIGHTS

The attitude of the U.S. legal system toward the rights of people receiving services has undergone a significant change in the last few decades. The courts used to assume that human services professionals always acted in the best interests of the people they served; therefore, those professionals were given unlimited power. That is no longer the case. This part of the chapter discusses the shift in underlying social assumptions that accompanied or caused changes in judicial attitudes about the law and human services.

The U.S. government relies on a balance of powers. The authors of the U.S. Constitution wished to prevent a situation that would permit any one person or institution to possess too much power. Consequently, they designed a government that spread power over three branches. Furthermore, the first 10 amendments of the U.S. Constitution, collectively known as the Bill of Rights, guarantee certain rights to all citizens. These are as follows.

Amendment I   Congress shall make no law respecting an establishment of religion, or prohibiting the free exercise thereof; or abridging the freedom of speech, or of the press; or the right of the people peaceably to assemble, and to petition the Government for a redress of grievances.

Amendment II   A well-regulated militia, being necessary to the security of a free State, the right of the people to keep and bear arms, shall not be infringed.

Amendment III   No soldier shall, in time of peace, be quartered in any house, without the consent of the owner, nor in time of war, but in a manner to be prescribed by law.

Amendment IV   The right of the people to be secure in their persons, houses, papers, and effects, against unreasonable searches and seizures, shall not be violated, and no warrants shall issue, but upon probable cause, supported by oath or affirmation, and particularly describing the place to be searched, and the persons or things to be seized.

Amendment V   No person shall be held to answer for a capital, or otherwise infamous crime, unless on a presentment or indictment of a Grand Jury, except in cases arising in the land or naval forces, or in the militia, when in actual service in time of war or public danger; nor shall any person be subject for the same offense to be twice put in jeopardy of life or limb; nor shall be compelled in any criminal case to be a witness against himself, nor be deprived of life, liberty, or property, without due process of law; nor shall private property be taken for public use, without just compensation.

Amendment VI   In all criminal prosecutions, the accused shall enjoy the right to a speedy and public trial, by an impartial jury of the State and district wherein the crime shall have been committed, which district shall have been previously ascertained by law, and to be informed of the nature and cause of the accusation; to be confronted with the witnesses against him; to have compulsory process for obtaining witnesses in his favor, and to have the assistance of counsel for his defense.

Amendment VII   In suits at common law, where the value in controversy shall exceed twenty dollars, the right of trial by jury shall be preserved, and no fact tried by a jury, shall be otherwise re-examined in any court of the United States, than according to the rules of the common law.

Amendment VIII   Excessive bail shall not be required, nor excessive fines imposed, nor cruel and unusual punishments inflicted.

Amendment IX   The enumeration in the Constitution, of certain rights, shall not be construed to deny or disparage others retained by the people.

Amendment X   The powers not delegated to the United States by
the Constitution, nor prohibited by it to the States, are reserved to the
States respectively, or to the people.

You have undoubtedly studied the Bill of Rights in history, political science, or civics classes. What you may not know is that people receiving a variety of human services have often not had the same rights
as typical U.S. citizens. In fact, "violations of individual rights that
would have created an instantaneous political and legal clamor had
they been perpetrated by the police went unrecognized when they
were perpetrated by social service professionals" (Glasser, 1981, p. 112).

One major example of a violation of individual rights is lack of access to due process. Until late in the 20th century, a person with mental retardation or a mental illness could be locked up for treatment and
automatically forbidden access to visitors, telephones, and attorneys.
There were no procedures for determining whether these restrictions
were necessary for treatment. This was possible because everyone assumed human services professionals always acted in the best interests
of the people they served.

The courts no longer assume that human services workers are always benevolent (Glasser, 1981). Instead, the courts often appear to assume that there is a conflict between the interests of service recipients
and the interests of the providers of those services (Rothman, 1981c).
This assumption may be hard for some human services professionals
to understand. After all, they became human services professionals to
help people. Why should anyone assume they are enemies rather than
friends? Following are three situations, based on actual cases, in which
human services workers did not appear to be acting in the client's best
interest.

In one instance, a vocational counselor worked with a young man
to develop a plan for getting a job. After the plan had been written, the
man changed his mind about the type of work he wanted to do. The
counselor was very upset with this change. Why? Because it meant re-
doing the required paperwork and thus meant more work for the
counselor.

In a second situation, a married couple was participating in a special apartment program that provided support services for people with
mental illnesses. One of the individuals started having problems that
were best helped with more intensive support than the apartment program typically provided. The solution offered by the program was un-
satisfactory: The couple was counseled to separate so that the person
having problems could move to a more intensive service program.

Another unfortunate situation occurred when a young man with
severe physical disabilities was placed in a sheltered workshop pack-

aging fish hooks. This is something one might do for the money, if nothing else was available, but one would be unlikely to choose this as a lifelong occupation. Imagine having cerebral palsy and having impairments so severe that one must use a wheelchair to go from place to place and a communication board to communicate. In addition, imagine having very limited motor control. This mismatch of job tasks and physical needs occurred because packaging fish hooks was the only available job in the workshop.

In the first example, the counselor was more concerned with the demands on her time than with her client's wishes. In the second example, the service program was willing to break up a marriage rather than adjust the manner of service delivery. In the third example, the agency used the job that was available rather than devising one that would be suited to the man's physical limitations. Each person was therefore put in a situation guaranteed to be frustrating and dehumanizing. No wonder the courts do not assume human services professionals always act in the best interests of the people they serve!

Christa Pavlus

> I think it's an ongoing learning process about what your clients' rights are. There are so many subtleties to it that you don't realize until you're in a certain setting, because they are different for different settings.

While serving as Executive Director of the American Civil Liberties Union, Ira Glasser proposed three principles for permitting social programs to function while limiting unintended negative consequences:

1. "The Bill of Rights applies to the human services and limits the powers of those services over the lives of the people being served" (1981, p. 127). For example, no one can have his or her rights abridged without due process of law.
2. "Enforcement of constitutional limits is not self-executing and therefore requires an external force" (1981, p. 136). Therefore, there is a need for outside advocates who help protect the rights of people receiving services.
3. "Every program designed to help the dependent ought to be evaluated, not on the basis of the good it might do, but rather on the basis of the harm it might do. Those programs ought to be adopted that seem to be the least likely to make things worse" (1981, p. 145).

These principles may seem harsh to you in your role as a professional member of the human services field. Consider them when you respond to the exercise in the following section. Then decide whether Glasser's principles still seem unreasonable.

HOW WOULD YOU WANT TO BE TREATED?

I still believe the emperor is wearing no clothes most of the time.

(Ellerbee, 1995, p. 61A)

People with physical disabilities sometimes refer to people without disabilities as being "temporarily able-bodied." This is a difficult concept for many of us to face because few of us are comfortable with the notion that someday we may not be able to do the things we do now. Of all the reasons we may someday need to receive human services, however, disability due to injury or illness is surely one of the most common.

Exercise

Suppose that while returning home from a dinner party at a friend's house, your car is hit by another car driven by someone who has had too much to drink. You wake up to find yourself in the hospital and have permanently lost the use of your legs.

2-10. Given the situation described above, do the research necessary to answer the following questions:
   a. What are your needs in all areas of life functioning (e.g., personal care, transportation, employment)?
   b. What resources in your community are available to help you meet those needs?
   c. Who would help you?
   d. How would you want to be treated?
   e. How would this injury affect your current personal and professional goals?

MORE TALES OF DISILLUSIONED DIANA

As Diana reads Exercise 2-10, she shakes her head. "That nearly happened to me, although my injury wasn't permanent. Last summer, I tripped while jogging and really tore up my knee and leg. I was in a cast for months, first in a wheelchair and then on crutches. People were very condescending toward me. They acted like my brain was in my knee, talked to me in simple words, offered—no, insisted—on assisting me, and usually made things worse.

"I quickly found out about limitations—like heavy doors to rest rooms that I couldn't pull open with crutches. I was lucky I had a roommate then who could help me at home. Grocery shopping was a nightmare, with kids crashing into me and people getting impatient and pushing past me. I nearly wiped out in the produce section because there was water on the floor and it was slippery.

"That experience sure gave me a feel for this exercise. Now, let's see about the rest of the questions in this exercise."

SECTION II

Human Services Professional

CHAPTER 3

Human Problems, Human Services Values
or
How Shall We Help?

OBJECTIVES

- Acknowledge that human problems have complex, multiple causes.

- Identify and avoid the pitfalls of blaming the victim and acting morally superior.

- Determine whether a particular service practices the five values described in this chapter.

- Identify how cultural and ethnic differences can affect the delivery of human services.

- Acknowledge that you may disagree with current social policy as practiced by your agency.

Mary, a single mother with three children younger than the age of 5, is on welfare. She tried to work full time, but she could not make enough money to pay for child care and other bills. She is very depressed.

Does Mary have a problem? If so, what is it? What solution would you recommend? How would you implement this solution? The ways in which human services professionals go about solving social problems depend in part on their values and assumptions. We usually have assumptions about the causes of social problems and opinions about effective solutions for those problems. This chapter describes some of the ways values and assumptions may affect the work of the human services professional.

Jennifer Echarte

I think there's a rule now that no matter how many children you have, as a single mother you're only allowed to get so much from welfare, the same amount no matter how many kids. They really are assuming that mothers have more children to get more money. They don't provide day care, and they don't provide birth control. They don't provide all the education that these women need.

CAUSES OF SOCIAL PROBLEMS

I understand that in the world there are people who are nuts. But I am also sure that the world can make people nuts.

(Goodman, 1981, p. 22)

Society engages in an ongoing discussion about what social problems exist and how they should be solved. In fact, a large part of the political process is devoted to that discussion. However, there is rarely, if ever, total agreement among citizens and government agencies about the causes of and desirable solutions for social problems. Consider, for example, these proposed solutions to Mary's situation:

- She needs affordable child care so that she can work.
- She needs to stop sleeping around and having children.
- She needs antidepressant medication.
- She needs to try harder.
- She needs psychotherapy.
- She needs a better job.

- She needs increased welfare benefits.
- She needs child support payments from the father of her children.
- She needs a society with values that make it acceptable and perhaps desirable for mothers of young children to receive government support to stay at home.
- She needs to use an effective method of birth control.

Each of these solutions is based on a different assumption about the causes of and solutions to what others see as Mary's problem, assumptions about some of the most controversial topics: work, sex, and parenting. We live in a culture that is full of contradictory assumptions and messages. One message is that individuals should "pull themselves up by their bootstraps" and improve their lot in life. Many people whose lives have improved significantly have the attitude that "I did it, so can they, and it's their fault if they don't." Another perhaps contradictory message is that we should help the "less fortunate," those who do not have the same advantages as others in terms of money, support, or education.

Cheryl Lammers

We say, "Oh you poor thing, you poor thing, you poor thing," and then suddenly we say "Goddamn you, why did you do this?" There's no gray area here. A kid steps over the line to 18, and now he's totally responsible for what he did, and he'd better be making the right choices. At what point do people go from victims to being totally responsible? Where is that point?

As of 1999, the United States is engaging in a massive restructuring of its welfare system. The changes are based on the assumption that no one who is able to work, including parents with small children, should receive lifelong public support. However, parents, usually women, who stay home with small children because they have partners who are financially able to support them are seen as responsible, not as part of a social problem. These kinds of mixed messages about social issues are an unavoidable part of living in a democratic society, and such messages add to the complexity of working in human services.

> *People, once you leave high school, most problems have no*
> *right or wrong answers, just the best possible solution*
> *under the present given circumstances.*
> *(Ivins, 1994, p. 48A)*

The reality of our social problems is always more complex than is evident in any one simple slogan or politically popular movement. Human services professionals recognize that how a person acts at any given time is determined by the person's innate biological characteristics, the person's current biological state, the person's history (e.g., education, upbringing, cultural background), and the person's current environment. How much each of these factors contributes to the origins of a particular problem varies from problem to problem. Consider, for instance, the causes of autism as compared with the origins of child abuse.

Autism

The cause of autism previously was identified as indifferent treatment from unresponsive mothers. Research, however, does not support this hypothesis. Instead, a strong biological relationship between organic damage and autism has been established (Happé, 1994). Although there is no cure for autism, good intervention and supports can help minimize the effects of autism so that people with autism can live successfully in their communities (Lovaas, 1987). The biological characteristics of the individual, rather than the parental relationship, are the most likely cause of autism.

Child Abuse

Whether a child will be abused is influenced by a large number of variables, the two most important being the parents' history and the child's current environment. Personal characteristics that place a parent at risk for abusing a child include the following: emotional disturbance, limited coping and problem-solving skills (especially when angry), low self-esteem, alcoholism or substance abuse, a history of having been abused or neglected as a child, being a stepparent, and lack of emotional attachment to the child. Limited parental resources are also risk factors, including low socioeconomic status, being a single parent, having a large number of children, having children close together in age, lacking social supports, and lacking social and parenting skills. Finally, the question remains as to why only *some* parents with these characteristics abuse or neglect their children. One possible answer is that they become trapped in negative interactions that cycle them ever closer to abusive behavior. In any case, it appears that child abuse is the result of a complex interaction of variables (Grimes, 1996).

Fitting Solutions to the Causes of Problems

Because autism and child abuse have different causes, they also require different approaches to their solutions. On the one hand, the long-term solution to autism is likely to be found by scientific study of the organic causes of autism and ways to prevent it. In the meantime, of course, we will need to provide services for people with autism that help them to lead fulfilling, productive lives. The long-term solution to child abuse, on the other hand, is not likely to be found in a laboratory filled with test tubes and equipment. Instead, the solution probably lies with how we teach people to parent, the type of supports society gives parents, and the penalties imposed for abusing a child. It is important for human services workers to know about the causes of the social problems they work on and the solutions that have been shown to be effective. This is the only way long-term solutions for these problems can be designed. It is also the only way to avoid two common pitfalls, blaming the victim and acting morally superior.

Exercise

3-1. Pick two problems currently being addressed by one of the human services fields (examples of problems might include teen pregnancy or older adults who cannot drive). For each problem, do the following:

  a. Ask a sampling of people from a variety of professions what they think causes those problems.

  b. Ask the same people to describe how to solve the problems.

  c. Look at some of the current professional literature on causes of the problems and recommended solutions.

  d. Describe the similarities and differences between the answers you obtained for 3-1a and 3-1b and those that you obtained for 3-1c.

  e. Do the solutions people recommend differ depending on what they say causes the problem?

TWO PITFALLS TO AVOID

All of us who work in human services always need to remain aware of the complex causes of human problems, new research findings on those causes, and our attitudes toward people with problems. In addition, we need to avoid what is probably the most common and most counterproductive pitfall in the field: *blaming the victim*. Blaming the victim involves suggesting a person is responsible for causing her own problems. For instance, a woman whose husband abuses her may be accused of doing something to deserve the abuse. Blaming the victim is rarely useful. Often the implied assumption is "You're responsible for the problem, so go fix it." If it were that simple, many people would have fixed their problems already without assistance. Also, blaming people for their own problems sometimes perpetuates the problem. Perpetrators of child sexual abuse, for example, often blame their victims, who then feel they have no right to complain.

I do not mean to suggest that recipients of human services have no part in the solutions to their problems. Even when people have problems they did not cause, they still have responsibility for active participation in the solutions. Active participation by recipients of human services is usually necessary to ensure the success of the service being offered. Expecting participation, however, is very different from blaming the victim or acting superior to those you help.

Another pitfall for professionals in the human services is the temptation *to feel and act morally superior* to the people whom one is supposed to serve because one does not have the same problems. If it is hard for you to imagine falling into this trap, then consider some typical reactions to smoking. People who have never smoked often cannot understand what anyone could possibly get out of that smelly habit and behave as though smokers may not have the right to exist at all. Ex-smokers may take the position "I quit, why can't you?" Smokers often swear that when they quit they will never be as self-righteous as some of the ex-smokers they know. Acting morally superior to someone with a problem is unlikely to lead to a solution to that problem. Few of us respond positively to being told what terrible, immoral people we are.

Exercises

3-2.   Ask people currently working in or receiving human services to describe situations in which they observed someone:
     a.   Blaming the victim
     b.   Acting morally superior
3-3.   Describe a situation in which someone acted morally superior to you. How did you feel when that happened?

> *A woman in prison on what she'd do differently:*
> *"Have money before children."*
> (Singleton, 1993b, p. 11B)

VALUES FOR THE HUMAN SERVICES

The type of service offered as a solution for a problem will vary depending on the nature of the problem. In the author's opinion, however, there are some underlying values applicable to all human services. These values are meant to serve as guidelines for interacting with clients and for designing effective services.

A Proactive Approach to Human Services

Most of the human services systems in the United States are reactive in nature. A problem occurs, so we try to solve it. People get sick, so we try to cure them. Crimes are committed, so we try to punish or rehabilitate the offenders. People do not have homes or jobs, so we try to help them find housing or employment. These are natural reactions; after all, if your home were on fire, you would try to put out the fire. However, if you want not only to solve the problem but also to prevent it from occurring again in the future, then reactive solutions are not enough—you need to design *proactive* solutions. A proactive approach to human problems is one that involves anticipating and preventing problems before they happen (Bernstein, Ziarnik, Rudrud, & Czajkowski, 1981; Ziarnik, 1980). This approach, however, is by no means universal. We are so used to reacting to problems instead of trying to prevent them that it is difficult to change. Also, we are still not as skilled in planning proactive programs as we might be. We have a great deal yet to learn about designing effective and proactive human services. Consequently we often design programs that are only partially proactive.

An example of a partially proactive human service is one that identifies parents who are at risk for becoming abusive and teaches them healthier ways to handle their children. In contrast, a completely proactive approach to child abuse would involve teaching people how to be nonviolent parents *before* they have children. For instance, the Home Visitation by Nurses program sends nurses to teach parenting skills to pregnant women at risk of having problems during childbirth. A 1997 study by Elliott identified the program as exemplary in preventing violence.

Focus on Results

Most of us want to be caring and understanding human services professionals. Caring, however, is no substitute for results. People who are hungry need food much more than they need understanding. People who are out of work are going to improve their financial situations and their self-esteem by getting jobs, not by getting counseling alone. It is therefore important to always focus your efforts on results.

Sometimes we know which programs are effective, and sometimes we do not. It can be difficult for human services professionals to focus on results rather than the process. Sometimes the results that people need are expensive or threatening in other ways to people with power or people invested in the status quo, so results are difficult to achieve. Early intervention programs, for instance, which are often very effective, can also be quite expensive. Sometimes effective solutions are simple, and it can be difficult for human services professionals to admit that. It is "hard on the ego to not be able to give the service we want, and hard to admit meaningful solutions are simpler than we try to make them" (C. Learned, personal communication, October 27, 1986).

Empower the People You Serve

> *Empowerment comes from teaching others things they can do to become less dependent on you.*
> *(Blanchard, Carlos, & Randolph, 1996, p. 64)*

> *The best caretaker offers a combination of challenge and support. . . . To be nurturant is not always to concur and comfort, to stroke and flatter and appease; often, it requires offering a caring version of the truth, grounded in reality. . . . Real caring requires setting priorities and limits.*
> *(Bateson, 1989, p. 155)*

A human services agency that assumes it is helping individuals that it regards as "poor unfortunates" is unlikely to encourage people to help themselves. It can make us feel wonderful to give a hungry person food. The giving of food, however, is a temporary solution. A more lasting solution is one that helps individuals to learn how to obtain food for themselves. If you feed people forever, then they are forever dependent. If you help them to feed themselves, then they will not always need human services to take care of them.

Many groups of people formerly thought to be forever dependent are now insisting on becoming sufficiently powerful and independent to care for themselves. For example, numerous people with severe physical disabilities have taken this position. Since the late 1960s, independent living centers have been established all over the country. These centers are run partly or completely by people with disabilities. Such centers help individuals with severe disabilities to live and work in local communities instead of in nursing homes or other restrictive settings.

Christa Pavlus

We have a lot to learn from them [the people we help]. We're not only here to teach them. They teach us. We're here to take care of people and sometimes we can get a lot from them too. I think that people forget that.

Empowerment and Control   It is hard to step back and help people make their own decisions when we strongly favor one choice in particular. It may be hard to help people make certain difficult decisions for themselves:

- Whether a pregnant 15-year-old should have an abortion
- Whether a man with mental retardation should take a job doing work he does not like because it pays well
- Whether an individual with AIDS should tell her parents about her diagnosis

Helping people to make their own decisions instead of telling them what to do is not easy. It is usually more time consuming, particularly when you are serving people who do not have much practice at making their own decisions. Depending on the skills a person already has, teaching decision making can involve one or more of the following steps:

- Figuring out that there is a decision to be made
- Generating several possible decisions from which to choose
- Analyzing possible outcomes of each decision
- Choosing the decision most likely to work for the decision maker

If one of your values is empowerment, you may need to learn to teach decision-making skills to the people you serve (see D'Zurilla, 1987). Also, you need to be able to monitor yourself and look for ways in which you can help people make their own decisions as well as ways in which you hinder their independent decision making.

Human services professionals who wish to empower the people they serve must not only avoid telling service consumers what to do but also avoid taking too much credit for improvements in people's lives. We all need to feel in control of our lives and are unlikely to react well to someone else claiming to have control over us.

Exercise

3-4.   In each of the following situations, how would you respond so that people will be encouraged to make their own decisions?

   a.   A student comes to the counseling center and says, "I've always wanted to be an English teacher, but lately I've been having second thoughts. Maybe I should go into business instead."

    b.   A man who has been living with a woman and their two children is trying to decide whether to propose to her.

    c.   A woman comes for help in deciding whether to tell her children that she is a lesbian.

Avoid Coercion

> *No one likes being told how to run his affairs.*
>
> *(Rothman, 1981a, p. 180)*

It can be hard to accept that some of the people we want to help do not want our help. Most people, however, have the right to refuse our services. The only exceptions are those individuals who are dangerous to themselves or to others. Such people include drunk drivers, abusive parents, and people with mental illnesses who are dangerous to themselves or others. In such cases, judges can order that services be administered. Otherwise services cannot be forced on anyone. Even people who are homeless and hungry cannot be forced to take our help.

An individual might choose to reject a service for many reasons, including the following: It is in conflict with the person's moral or religious standards; it is too costly in terms of the time, the money, or the effort required; it might have undesirable side effects; it might restrict the individual's freedom; or it simply is not wanted. One possible response to objections such as these is to redesign your service, a topic that is beyond the scope of this book. Do keep in mind, however, that services can sometimes be made less costly for and more compatible with the needs of consumers.

Be Sensitive to Diversity

The members of our society come from diverse cultures, religions, and value systems. One of the hard questions facing any human services professional is determining a way to solve a particular social problem that is both effective and considerate of this diversity. In fact, it may not be possible for a human services professional to be effective without addressing this issue.

Jennifer Echarte

I think I've had some cultural problems because when I was growing up, affection was always something that was always part of our interactions. Touch and contact were welcomed, and when you met a stranger you kissed them, sometimes twice, on the cheek. The boundaries are very different, and I've gotten into some problems because of having contact with people. There was this one episode where an adolescent boy was wearing a collar, a dog collar that would fit my dog. I took the collar and looped my finger and said, "What is this?" I pulled on it because we had that rapport where I could joke around with him. It was a behavioral treatment center, and somebody saw this and turned me in. I got into a lot of trouble for having any contact. I feel that a lot of times that contact, that hug, or that pat on the back is something that makes people feel accepted and makes people feel part of something, and I've constantly been reprimanded.

The recent news coverage of efforts to stop the spread of AIDS provides an example of the ways in which diverse values affect decisions about solving social problems. Some religious groups are encouraging abstinence from both drug use and sexual activity as a way to prevent AIDS and are opposed to needle exchange programs and safer sex education. Other medical, religious, and political groups favor needle exchange programs and education of individuals who are sexually active about ways to reduce exposure to AIDS. These groups point to evidence that needle exchange and safer sex education programs reduce the incidence of AIDS. This disagreement is clearly related to diverse moral and religious convictions within our society.

People and organizations are being insensitive to diversity when they assume that their way of doing things is the "normal" way and that everyone they serve should try to be more "normal." Following are some of the ways you can increase your sensitivity to diverse cultures, values, and habits:

1. Determine whether the people you serve belong to cultural, religious, or ethnic groups with which you are unfamiliar.
2. Examine the schedule and policies of your agency to determine whether they accommodate the people you serve. For instance, is the schedule sensitive to holidays that are important to consumers of your services?
3. If you serve people who speak limited English and are fluent in another language, then find out whether any of your staff speak that language.
4. Consider the diversity of your staff with respect to gender, ethnicity, age, disability, sexual orientation, and religious or spiritual affiliation.
5. Encourage a good working relationship between your agency and local community groups that represent the interests of specific ethnic, religious, or other diverse groups.

6. Examine the reading material in your agency's waiting rooms or public areas and the pictures on its walls. Are the people you serve represented in the magazines and the art hanging in the waiting rooms or the public areas of the agency? Are there reading materials or artworks that might be offensive to members of certain groups?

7. Consider whether any of the goals of your agency are in conflict with the values of any of the people you serve. Do you have enough information to answer this question? If there is a conflict, then how is your agency dealing with that conflict? (adapted from Nicoloff, 1985)

Cathy Phelps

I try to practice what I preach. I am impatient when other people do not. For instance, on the issue of recruiting and hiring people of color to work in this field: I get tired of being told, "We can't find anybody, we can't hire anybody." That happens when we always look in the same places. We post in the same paper, we never step outside the box, we don't go to the school of anthropology, we don't look in business, we just look in psychology or social work, or we look for the same type of person that is already the kind of person we have in our agencies. People of color are offered the same roles: administrative assistant or outreach coordinator, never volunteer manager or executive director.

Also, I feel like if you can't find them [diverse staff] then you grow them. At the agency I'm currently at we've been pretty successful with that, but it does require a different level, I think, of investment. I don't mean unfairly discriminating against another group of people. But I mean that you have your vision, and you try to work toward that. If that means reposting a job several times; if it means looking at who you are as an agency; if it means asking people about what they believe your agency is, what your agency's role is, or how you're perceived in the community, then you do it.

Exercises

3-5. Describe the human services field in which you work or hope to work. What information do you have that tells you whether this field is

     a.   Proactive?

     b.   Results-oriented?

     c.   Empowering?

     d.   Sensitive to diversity?

3-6. Ask someone who works in your chosen form of human services what that field does to be sensitive to diversity.

3-7. Review the seven ways to increase sensitivity to diversity described previously. Identify up to three methods that are needed in your workplace or school and develop a plan for implementing at least one of them. If possible, carry out your plan.

CONFLICTS ABOUT VALUES IN HUMAN SERVICES

Human services professionals are expected to be especially skilled in solving certain social problems. For example, it is assumed they know how to coordinate services, change behavior, advocate, counsel, provide therapy, and connect people with needed resources. Often, however, public laws and outdated policies dictate the goals of the service professional. Sometimes personal opinions about desirable social goals do not agree with the goals set by the agencies that employ these professionals.

For instance, you might work for a public health agency as a social worker. Suppose the agency requires that anyone who comes in to be tested for a sexually transmitted disease give his name. Now suppose you believe more people would come in for testing and treatment if they could be tested anonymously. What do you do?

The goals of human services programs are often influenced by political and budgetary decisions. For example, federal legislators decide how much to spend on various national programs. The amount of money allocated for a particular program determines how many staff the program can afford to hire as well as how much it can spend on other resources such as buildings and materials.

More specific budget decisions made by program administrators also determine the policies of particular agencies. A school superintendent, for example, has to decide how much to allocate to each specialized program, such as classes for children who are gifted. A prison director has to decide how much to allocate to new buildings, educational programs, or salaries.

As mentioned previously, you sometimes may disagree with your agency's policy (or legislation that sets policy). There is no right or wrong answer to the question of how to handle policy disagreements you have with your employer. If the disagreement is extreme, you may wish to resign rather than live with a policy that you oppose. Less drastic measures might include lobbying with your administration and/or congressional representatives for a change in the policy. You may do this individually or through a political action or advocacy group. All citizens of a democracy have the opportunity to contribute to decisions about social policy.

Exercise

3-8.   If you are currently working in human services, then how do you deal with your disagreements, if any, with your agency's policies? If you are currently a student, then ask one of your instructors to invite human services professionals to your class to discuss this question.

MORE TALES OF DISILLUSIONED DIANA

Several weeks later, Diana and some of her friends meet at her apartment. She has been sharing *"Human services? . . . That must be so rewarding."* with them; now they meet regularly to talk through the exercises and their experiences and give each other support.

Akram, a friend of Diana's who works in a residential treatment home for children, says, "This month's exercises really hit home. I had a major disagreement with my supervisor over the agency's decision to cut the number of staff on the night shift. I know our budget is tight, but it's really dangerous for the other kids and the staff if there aren't enough of us to handle physical aggression safely." The group's conversation escalates into a heated discussion of this policy. Finally Diana asks, "What can we or Akram do?" After more discussion, Akram decides to approach his supervisor in a more rational way than he has in the past, because his earlier ranting and raving have not worked. He plans to ask for support in getting the decision changed through educating policy makers about the program's staffing needs. Diana and the other group members offer to lend support and speak up as concerned citizens.

SECTION III

Human Services Professional

IN PERSPECTIVE

Most of this book is about what human services workers need to do to be effective. However, no one works in a vacuum. Before proceeding to the specifics of this section, consider the context in which human services professionals work. We need three types of resources in order to be effective. They are as follows:

1. **Information**   We need to know the following information:
   - The goals of the agency where we work: What is the agency supposed to accomplish? What are its values?
   - Our responsibilities: What are we supposed to accomplish? How are these accomplishments supposed to contribute to achievement of the goals of the organization?
   - The methods we are expected to use: How are we supposed to achieve the desired results? Are there certain approaches that are required and others that we may not use?

2. **Resources**   The resources we have consist of the following things:
   - Our skills: Most of this book addresses some of the skills we need.
   - Materials: Several familiar examples include buildings, food, library materials, and a telephone.

3. **Consequences**   We have to know whether the things we do make any difference, and we need rewards for doing a good job. Specifically, the consequences we need are as follows:
   - Feedback: We all need clear, frequent, and specific feedback that tells us what we have done well and what we need to do differently.
   - Rewards: The most common reward in the human services is praise for doing a good job. It can come from consumers of your services, from your supervisors, or from your colleagues. Few of us feel good about our work without some sort of reward (Gilbert, 1978).

Most of this book concerns your skills, but skills alone are not enough. You still need good information and sufficient consequences in order to be effective. The best time to evaluate whether you have enough information to do a good job is when you are interviewing for a position (see Chapter 7). The question of whether sufficient consequences are available will come up in the discussion of interviewing and again in Chapter 8 (on stress management). So, as you read this section, remember that the skills discussed here are only part of what you need to do good work.

CHAPTER 4

Professional Relationships
or
People Who Need People

OBJECTIVES

- Describe how to have good relationships with other staff in your agency.

- Describe how to have good relationships with staff of other agencies.

Effective human services professionals are able to develop and maintain good relationships with a wide variety of people. This is not surprising. After all, most human services work involves people and how they interact. Training in the human services tends to focus on relationships with consumers of services, with good reason. If you are to be effective in serving people, however, you also need skills in working effectively with colleagues, supervisors, and professionals from other agencies. This chapter describes some basic components of good relationships with other professionals (except for communication, which is covered in Chapter 6).

WORKING RELATIONSHIPS: GENERAL GUIDELINES

> *Small decencies are excellent tell tales. Their absence screams of personal disrespect, harried and overworked people, a harsh or cold atmosphere, an environment corrosive to the human spirit. Their presence almost infallibly suggests caring, time for thought and reflection, and attention to the needs of people beyond the need for a cup of hot coffee.*
> *(Cowan, 1992, p. 18)*

Human services professionals who are good at maintaining positive relationships follow five basic guidelines.

1. *They treat everyone with respect and common courtesy.* They remember to take the time to thank people, to listen carefully, and to be polite, even to those with whom they disagree (courtesy is not the same as agreement). For a more detailed and humorous description of the basics of common courtesy, see *Miss Manners' Guide to Excruciatingly Correct Behavior* (Martin, 1991). One important part of courtesy is returning telephone calls and responding to e-mail requests as quickly as possible.
2. *They do what they say they will do.* They follow through on commitments. If for some reason they are unable to follow through, they tell you that there is a problem and make an attempt to compensate. They also tell you what they cannot do, and they do not make commitments they know they cannot keep. They are reliable and are on time for appointments and meetings. If they are running late, they call and tell you as far in advance as possible.
3. *They are proactive.* They focus their efforts on how to anticipate and solve problems, or parts of problems, before those problems occur. They do not emphasize how awful things are and how many problems they cannot solve. They emphasize strengths in people and organizations.

4. *They check their facts.* They do not rely on hearsay or gossip, and they routinely obtain information from several different sources before taking a position on an issue or taking action.
5. *They are accountable for what they do.* They acknowledge their failures as well as their successes. When they make mistakes, they admit to them and learn from them.

Exercise

4-1. Describe how a human services worker who works well with others would handle each of the following situations:
   a. Your supervisor tells you there is a mandatory meeting of the entire staff in 2 hours. You have already scheduled a meeting at that time with staff from three other agencies.
   b. A speech-language therapist from another agency calls and tells you he has heard that an individual whom you both serve is starting to miss work and use drugs. He is calling to say he is ready to report this person for parole violations.
   c. One of your colleagues constantly complains that there is too much paperwork, so much that she cannot do a good job of providing services. You have noticed that there do seem to be a large number of forms to fill out.

Possible Solution to Exercise 4-1a

Explain your conflict to your supervisor. If you are told you must be at the staff meeting, call the other agencies. Explain that a mandatory emergency meeting has been called, make a sincere apology, and ask the other agencies to have the meeting without you or to reschedule it. If the meeting will be rescheduled, be ready to provide specific times you are available. Repeat your apology, and end the conversation. Do not refer to your supervisor or the emergency meeting as inflexible or unreasonable, even if they are. This solution is proactive: It allows you to maintain a positive relationship with your supervisor and the other agencies. It does not, however, guarantee a positive relationship with others who are inflexible or unreasonable.

WORKING WITH COLLEAGUES: SUPPORT STAFF

Too often administrative assistants, secretaries, janitors, and other support staff are treated with little respect and are not seen as professionals. This is unfortunate for several reasons. First, and most important, it is incumbent upon us to practice what we preach. If we truly believe that all people are entitled to be treated with respect, to be asked for input about decisions that affect them, and to have their contributions to the world acknowledged, then we need to behave in ways that reflect this belief all the time. There is no excuse for being rude to support staff or for failing to include them in discussions of changes relevant to them, nor is there any excuse for only acknowledging their contributions to the agency once a year (on Secretaries' Day, for example), if at all.

The people who answer your telephones (if people do indeed answer your telephones) and clean your offices make it possible for you to do your job. They are entitled, as we all are, to recognition for a job well done and to respect and courtesy as a matter of course. Saying "Please" and "Thank you" not only recognizes the respect to which everyone is entitled but also contributes to a more pleasant working atmosphere. Finally, your support staff are probably going to provide better services when they are treated with respect than when they are not. You should not, however, expect special favors just because you are courteous to support staff. For instance, do not expect someone to stay late to help you with a project you have put off until the last minute. This is an abuse of power and an example of expecting someone else to clean up your mess. Furthermore, doing so is unacceptable behavior on the part of any adult, let alone any human services professional.

Exercises

4-2. Identify three ways to recognize and reward contributions of support staff to your organization throughout the year. Do not use flowers, candy, or anything specific to Secretaries' Day.

4-3. Identify three ways to help support staff feel important to and involved in organizational planning and operations.

WORKING WITH COLLEAGUES: OTHER PROFESSIONALS

Suzanne Cardiff

I like working with teams. I think that's a huge, huge thing in social services. You have to work in a team, or nobody gets anything done. Everybody's got so many different jobs, and you can't get anything done without all those people doing those jobs. So, one person slacks, and it's the whole team that suffers. By "team" I mean not just your unit, but different departments that have to do different things for that one case.

Heidi Daly

Working with teams, I've always felt very challenged by it, but I've also found it very rewarding because it really is the point of being in a medical setting. You work with different aspects of it like with the nursing, the physical therapy, the occupational therapy, all of the people that work with the patients. They see different things about the patients than the social worker does. The social worker is only with the patients a few minutes a week, and the nursing aides, the nurses, everybody is definitely more in touch with them, so you get a lot of information from them, more so than what you would find by yourself.

Pamela Meister

For me, I've had the comparison of having worked in the sales arena for so long. That's such a competitive team to work with. It's not really a team, it's kind of "I can do a little more than you; I'm gonna try and impress the boss." What I've found in the social services area is that it is "Let's all work together, how can we come up with a solution," and it's less self-focused.

I came in here [the hospital], and we were in a meeting. One of the issues was housing for families of transplant patients and [people said] "What are we gonna do? Let's solve this problem together." There was compassion and caring, and it was so different, to see that. We didn't really have an answer, but we'd brainstormed on ideas.

Christa Pavlus

It's a matter of learning what the needs are of the people that work with you and finding out what works for them, what are their best communication styles, how do I let them know what I need. Everything that everybody does is very important. Sometimes it's difficult to step outside of yourself for a minute and ask if I need to consider what these other people are doing, what kinds of things are holding them back, what kinds of walls they're running into in terms of their schedules, their staffing.

I think when you come out of school you don't want to step on anybody's toes. I was always afraid to say what I really felt because I didn't want anybody upset with me. I have learned not everybody is going to be happy with me all the time. Even if you want to be friends with everybody all the time, it's not going to happen. For my patients' benefit, I've had to learn to feel confident in telling co-workers what my concerns are, saying it without sounding meek but also without sounding like I'm placing blame. I think that that's an important skill to have 'cause otherwise it's very easy to jump down people's throats. You have to learn to take a moment and first find out what's going on in their situation but also let them know what you need. That's not always going to hurt somebody's feelings, and sometimes if it does that's too bad.

Johnn Young

Working with teams is a good thing. I work with a team in the education department here of about eight of us, and when we pull together around one common issue, it flows. It's like being in the theater, because when everything flows and when it works well, everybody knows their parts, everybody knows what they're supposed to say and when they're supposed to say it. It all just fits, and it flows, and you can see the pieces come together.

The development of good working relationships with other human services professionals within your agency is one of the most difficult tasks that you face. When we work closely with people over a long period of time, they come to know our strengths and our faults well. We come to know theirs equally well. It is easy, but not very useful, to focus on what our colleagues do badly. We all have characteristics that other people find irritating or frustrating, such as popping chewing gum, being chronically late to meetings, overemphasizing minor problems, or speaking with a voice that others find too loud or too soft.

An emphasis on your co-workers' strengths is more difficult, but also more rewarding, than an emphasis on their faults. Furthermore, none of us is perfect, so we are probably just as annoying to them as they are to us! One of the ways to build positive working relationships is to look on these relationships as being collaborative (Zins, 1985). In collaborative relationships, each individual contributes in her areas of strength and seeks assistance from others who have skills in other areas.

For instance, suppose you are very good at working with people once they come to you for services, but you are not good at going into new situations and letting people know what you have to offer. This is an ideal opportunity to build a collaborative relationship with a colleague who is good at presenting your agency to potential users of services. It is important for other people to feel you need them, and it is important that you do not present yourself as an expert in everything. No one knows everything, and people who act as though they do are usually treated with hostility and suspicion.

It is particularly important to build good working relationships with your colleagues when your work often requires you to be out of the office. Lack of visibility, which occurs when your colleagues do not have a chance to observe you doing the most important parts of your job, frequently leads to problems in human services agencies. When others do not see you working, they may assume you are not working. This is not because people always assume the worst. It is an invisibility problem: If a person does not see something and does not hear about it, then he tends to assume it does not exist. The solution to this problem is simple: Keep people informed about what you do. People who are interested in having good working relationships and keeping colleagues informed make sure their offices know how to reach them when they are out in the field. In addition, they take the time to sit down with colleagues who have mutual interests or overlapping responsibilities and say things such as "I'm involved in a project in which you might be interested. Can I take a few minutes to fill you in?"

Exercises

4-4a. Identify five characteristics of your own that your colleagues might find irritating or unacceptable. How do you want your colleagues to deal with your quirks?

   b. Identify five characteristics of current or potential colleagues that you find irritating or unacceptable. How should you deal with theirs?

4-5. Describe three ways in which you could demonstrate respect for a colleague's skills.

4-6. Think about successful relationships between colleagues that you have observed. Describe how the people involved treat each other.

SUPERVISION

Our supervisors connect us with the organizations in which we work. It is often difficult to develop a good relationship with a supervisor because many of us have some difficulty in our relationships with people in positions of authority. Working with supervisors can be touchy because they evaluate your performance, and we sometimes respond by avoiding supervisors whenever possible. That avoidance is understandable but not very useful.

On Being Supervised

There are ways you can act if you want to have a positive relationship with your supervisor and ways your supervisor can work positively with you. The supervisory relationship does not have to be a negative one.

You have several obligations to your supervisor:

- Keep your supervisor informed about what you are doing and about any events that may be important to your organization.
- When you have a complaint about your organization, take it to your supervisor, not your colleagues. Remember, your supervisor may not agree with you, may not be able to solve the problem as quickly as you would like, or may not be able to solve it at all.
- Behave and expect to be treated as a professional, not a child. Supervisors are not parents.
- Treat your supervisor with respect even if you do not think it is deserved. It helps to like the people you work with, but it is not essential. Treating your supervisor and your colleagues with respect is essential.
- Give your supervisor positive, constructive criticism on how you are being supervised. Remember to use diplomacy. Be aware that all supervisors may not be open to constructive criticism.
- Remember your supervisor is your supervisor, with responsibilities to both you and the organization. Expect your supervisor to have a professional relationship with you, not a close friendship.

Here are two helpful ways to approach developing a positive relationship with your supervisor. First, treat your supervisor as a consumer. Use tact and timing in presenting issues to your supervisor, just as you would with other important people in your life. If your supervisor gives you feedback you do not fully understand, ask for clarification. Use the type of communication (e.g., memo, face-to-face meeting) and schedule for communicating preferred by your supervisor (Scott, 1990).

Second, try to see things from your supervisor's perspective: Try to mirror your supervisor's need to see the big picture. Be sensitive to the multiple demands on your supervisor's time, and keep in mind that every little detail of your daily work is not of interest to her. Prepare carefully for meetings with your supervisor. Try to present issues and reports that cover important points as briefly as possible (but be prepared to provide more detail in case it is requested). If you have problems to present, then be prepared to suggest at least one solution. Even when your solution is not used, the fact that you have provided one shows that you are committed to being an active part of the problem-solving process (Murphy, 1987).

On Being a Supervisor

If you make human services your career for an extended period of time, then you will almost certainly become a supervisor. Just as you have obligations to the person who is your supervisor, you have obligations to the people you supervise.

You have several obligations to the people you supervise:

- Be accessible.
- Practice what you preach. If your staff are expected to treat service consumers and colleagues with respect and with some understanding of their problems, they have a right to receive similar treatment from their supervisor.
- Make clear what is expected of your staff professionally (Blanchard et al., 1996). These expectations should be tempered by a realistic view of available resources (McInerney, 1985).
- Treat your staff with respect, even when they disagree with you (McInerney, 1985).
- Give staff members regular, specific feedback about work performance. This does not refer to semiannual or annual reviews, but rather to ongoing daily or weekly comments about what they are doing well and what needs improvement. People who do not get useful feedback cannot be expected to perform well (Blanchard et al., 1996). They also have the right to expect recognition for a job well done.
- Everyone you supervise has the right to make mistakes and learn from them (McInerney, 1985).
- Guarantee the right to confidentiality regarding supervision, particularly when giving constructive criticism (McInerney, 1985). Effective supervisors provide praise in public and constructive criticism in private.
- Learn how to supervise effectively. Human services professionals often are promoted to supervisory positions because they work well with clients. This does not automatically mean they have good supervision skills.

Mary Anne Harvey

One of the things I also find as a manager is that I don't have as much patience as I used to have. I want people to take responsibility for their own lives and their own feelings. I understand that when people come into an organization and just because of the position I happen to have, there's a lot of mother stuff that gets transferred to me. I have no patience for that any more. I really want people who work here to be happy to be here, and if they're not, I really want to support them in going somewhere where they will be happy. Our work is too hard, and it's too important to have people making turmoil for the organization, and that's sometimes what happens. We do a lot of teaching in our work and our supervision—a lot more than I think I expected to do. I'm not as patient about some things, and I try very hard not to reinforce certain kinds of behavior.

Christa Pavlus

I've learned that it is important to know how to delegate. I used to be the kind of person who felt I had to do everything, and of course I think that the way I do everything is the best way and the right way. It's very hard to learn to let go of those things, but it can become very overwhelming when you have a lot to do. It's very important to learn to delegate. Things may not get done exactly the way I would have done it, but that doesn't mean it's the wrong way. That has been one of my biggest things, to be able to turn to someone and say, "Okay, I'm feeling a little overwhelmed, can you help with this?"

WORKING WITH STAFF AT OTHER AGENCIES

Ellen Berlin

Whatever the class might be, a skills class in a community agency, a school, or a morning school, we go in 1 day a week. So when you go in anywhere 1 day a week, you're really just a visitor, but you need their space. You need to have a working relationship 1 day a week, and you need the secretary who answers the telephone to know you have a program there so she can be a resource, and the school nurse, and the school psychologist. It's just always an interesting situation of juggling all those needs because we're supposed to keep a sense of some kind of peace. Anybody who works in this job—if they do not learn flexibility in the first week, they don't stay.

Suzanne Cardiff

I haven't had any problem working with other agencies. Most of the agencies that I can think of right now have been totally cooperative and helpful. If they can't help me, they find somebody who can.

Heidi Daly

Finding the right agency for the person is probably the biggest challenge because there's just some that don't do what the patient needs. They will only work 1 day a week with them, or they will only do so much with them in their home. Or the audiologist or the eye doctor may not come to the nursing home, and you cannot get the patient out. That's a major obstacle.

Cathy Phelps

I remember having a conversation a couple of years ago with some providers at another agency. We were trying to work on developing a collaborative resource directory, and I spoke about the people that we served as clients and said that we did case management, which meant that we would recontact someone to say, "How are you doing, did those referrals work out, what else can we help with?" The people at the table were offended by that. They said they didn't have "clients," they had consumers and said what about confidentiality, what about empowerment. Well, I feel like we're a confidential agency, we get permission to recontact people, we get their permission to contact other agencies on their behalf. I'm as much of a feminist, as committed to empowerment as everybody else sitting at that table, but I felt like the language they were using and the method that we were using came into conflict. When we sat at that table I just thought, "Oh my God, we can't get past this?"

Trying to stay client-centered, which might mean to me that we have to put aside our territory, our turf issues, our funding competitiveness so that we can agree to work collaboratively with the client, sometimes it's difficult to do that because they don't want to tell us who she is. If we all work together and did what each of us do well versus trying to expand into areas that are beyond our mission, beyond our scope, we would do people a better service.

You really do a disservice to your clients and yourself professionally when you don't have very clear boundaries.

Johnn Young

I remember a time a while ago, we were working with other agencies around some prevention stuff. One agency took their information back to the board of directors and the board of directors decided they couldn't work out of their box. That was so disheartening because the work would have been important, we would have reached a lot of people together, it would have been a good thing.

Sometimes working with other agencies is a good thing because you can expand your resources and do more. It's getting to the point that the grantors and the federal government require you to play well together, so we're learning to get along, whether we want to or not.

Exercise

4-6. For each of the following situations, provide at least two ways to respond. Give responses that are likely to lead to a solution of the problem and are likely to maintain a good relationship with the other agency involved.

a. You are an independent living skills instructor for people with physical disabilities who are seeking jobs. One of the people you have been serving for some time announces that he is withdrawing from your program because his pastoral counselor told him the government will take care of him for the rest of his life, so he does not have to learn to do anything for himself.

b. You are a teacher of children with emotional disturbances. A representative from a local advocacy organization calls you on behalf of the Cohens, parents of one of the children you teach. The representative states that the Cohens want to have a special meeting to talk about improving the educational services being provided for their daughter. They feel the present program is not meeting their child's needs.

Possible Solutions to Exercise 4-6

a. You could say you agree it is true that the young man's government benefits will continue. Talk to him briefly about the self-worth many people gain from increasing their ability to care for themselves (but do not preach). Then give him your card, and tell him you will be glad to talk to him again if he changes his mind. Remember you have no way of knowing whether he is quoting his counselor accurately, so call that person and report what happened in a matter-of-fact way (if you have your client's consent to do so), and ask whether the quote is accurate. If it is accurate, then you may want to disagree, but do so directly with the pastoral counselor, not indirectly through the gossip mill.

b.   Check with the Cohens, and make sure they have authorized the advocate to represent them. Agree to have the requested meeting with the Cohens. Prepare for the meeting by summarizing the data you have concerning their daughter's identified needs and what the school program is doing for this child. Finally, listen carefully at the meeting before responding at all.

INTIMATE RELATIONSHIPS

There is usually no prohibition against intimate relationships with colleagues in the way that there is against sexual relationships with consumers of services. Having an intimate relationship with a colleague is still problematic, however, and may lead to conflict in the workplace. If other colleagues find out, and you value your privacy, discovery is a problem. Also, if your colleagues find out about the relationship, then they may have reactions you find objectionable, such as the expectation that you will keep them up to date on all the emotional details; jealousy, if you are involved with someone in whom they have an interest; moral condemnation; or matchmaking (trying to push the relationship into more intimacy and commitment than is desired). Another consideration is that you will still have to work with each other if the relationship ends, which can be very awkward.

Intimate relationships with professionals from other agencies may lead to similar problems. In addition, if the intimate relationship ends but the professional one must continue, then your agency's relationship with the other agency may be adversely affected.

Relationships between service delivery professionals and support staff may lead to different types of difficulties. If one of the people involved has more power than the other and the relationship ends, then the more powerful one may retaliate. This is unethical, but it does happen.

Moral condemnation and/or gossip are likely and can create considerable unpleasantness. A relationship that you find rewarding may be seen by others as sinful, unprofessional, or in bad taste. Should this occur, do not count on colleagues who hold these opinions to keep them a secret. This is particularly true if you are a woman. Although social values have changed in the last few decades, women are still judged more harshly than men for similar behavior. This is not desirable, but it does occur, and you need to be prepared for it.

Moral condemnation and/or gossip are also likely if your intimate relationships are with members of the same sex. Again, although some social values have changed, bisexual people, gay men, lesbians, and transgendered people are still more likely than their heterosexual colleagues to encounter negative attitudes.

The author is not suggesting that your social life never include your co-workers. It is usually not possible to divide life into such clean, neat categories. Do try, however, to remember the potential for problems when the irresistible woman or man in the next office asks you out for dinner.

ETHICAL ISSUES

One of the most difficult situations a human services professional can encounter is one in which a colleague is behaving unethically. For instance, a colleague might choose an intervention that is convenient but not necessarily designed to meet the client's needs (Fisher, 1995), or a support staff member might violate confidentiality. Deciding what to do when you see this sort of behavior is not easy. Solutions to ethical dilemmas are rarely simple, and you may feel torn between maintaining good working relationships and doing what you think is right. You may be reluctant to speak up about unethical behavior because you know whistle blowers sometimes lose their jobs. Some professional organizations have ethics committees that provide confidential consultation about ethical dilemmas. If your professional organization does not have such a committee, then you may want to suggest that one be created.

Seeing someone from another agency behaving unethically presents you with a different situation. You have to decide whether to address the issue, and if so, with whom you should speak. It is probably best to consult your supervisor before taking action.

NEGOTIATION

A wise agreement can be defined as one which meets the legitimate interests of each side to the extent possible, resolves conflicting interests fairly, is durable, and takes community interests into account.
(Fisher, Ury, & Patton, 1991, p. 4)

Negotiate means "to communicate on a matter of disagreement between two parties, with a view first to the other party's perspective and then to attempt to arrive at a resolution by consensus" (World Wide Legal Information Association, 1998). Thus, any conversations we have with other people that are intended to result in delivery of some human service are forms of negotiation. Principled negotiation, a process described by Fisher et al. (1991) of the Harvard Negotiation Project, can be particularly useful. Principled negotiation is concerned with both the substance and the process of negotiation. The concern with substance ensures that the result of a negotiation will, as much as possible, meet the legitimate interests of all those involved. The concern with process ensures that the negotiation process and its outcome will not damage the relationship between the people involved (Fisher et al., 1991).

Principled negotiation focuses on the interests or principles of the people involved, instead of on the people themselves or on particular positions. The intent is to find a solution consistent with the values of all concerned. In this way, it is possible for all negotiating parties to be winners; no one will lose.

Principled negotiation also assumes that the process by which you arrive at an agreement is as important as the substance of the agreement. If you want people to implement an agreed on solution to a problem, then you must ensure that they feel the solution is fair, and you must ensure that they feel they were important to the design of the solution. Following are some ways to make the negotiation process an effective one.

1. Use the language of social cohesion. Unoriginal remarks such as "How about this weather?" or "Did you catch that game last night?" may sound silly to you, but they serve several purposes. First, they establish a connection between people, so that when serious negotiations begin, those involved do not feel as though they are dealing with strangers. Also, they serve to establish a positive connection by allowing people who may later disagree or become angry with each other to discuss neutral, all-purpose topics. They keep communication open: Even when substantive discussions are at a standstill, people can stay in contact by discussing yesterday's record snowfall. Finally, unoriginal remarks can be useful because they prevent silence, and many people are uncomfortable with silence (Hayakawa, Hayakawa, & MacNeil, 1991).

> *If they are not involved in the process, they are hardly*
> *likely to approve the product.*
>
> *(Fisher et al., 1991, p. 27)*

2. Make sure everyone participates so that everyone has a stake in the solution. Negotiation must be approached without a specific solution in mind that is the only solution you will accept. Certainly, you will have some ideas about what is at stake and possible ways to proceed, but the other parties to the negotiation will also have ideas about what to do. The negotiation process should provide ways to combine those ideas and to find a solution acceptable to all concerned.

3. *Show appreciation for others' difficulties.* You may take it for granted that you understand the pressures and constraints felt by others, but they will not know you understand unless you tell them (Zins, 1985). For instance, you might say to a single parent, "It must be difficult for you to arrange to bring Thea in for regular therapy and still manage your work schedule and your son's after-school activities." Or, you might say to the rehabilitation counselor who works for the state office, "It sounds like you feel the bureaucratic requirements you need to meet will slow down the service delivery process." Note that in this example, you acknowledge the counselor's position without necessarily agreeing with it. People with whom you disagree need to know that you have heard them, even if you then disagree. Other parties to a negotiation will not listen if you ignore any expression with which you disagree.

4. *Arrange a physical environment that fosters cooperation.* It can help if two parties with differing interests sit on the same side of the table (Fisher et al., 1991; Lynch & Hanson, 1998). Round tables can also help. Avoid any arrangement that puts the consumer and his representatives on one side of a table and all the services providers on the other side (unless there are compelling cultural reasons to do so). Such an arrangement suggests that people have chosen sides and can make them more likely to behave as enemies.

5. *Accommodate cultural differences.* Different cultures vary with respect to the timing of negotiations, formality, how physical space and contact are used, relative emphasis on oral versus written agreements, the directness of communications, where negotiations occur, how relationships are established, and a host of other variables (Fisher et al., 1991; Lynch & Hanson, 1998). These sorts of differences occur among people within countries as well as internationally and must be accommodated if negotiations are to be successful.

6. *Explain your interests, and ask for theirs.* Do not assume that other parties understand your primary interest, and, even more important, do not assume you understand theirs. For instance, suppose you work in a residential program for children with emotional disturbances. One of the children has made considerable progress, and you are ready to recommend a less restrictive intervention environment (probably his home) to his parents. When meeting with them you could say, "My pri-

mary interest here is in finding a way for Jake to move to a more independent setting. We think he can function very well in his neighborhood school if the therapist consults with you and the teacher. You seem pleased with Jake's progress but reluctant to move him home. Could I ask you to describe your concerns?"

7. *Identify the problem before the answer.* Perhaps the single most important barrier to problem solving in human services is the tendency of many of us to assume we know what the problem is and, therefore, assume that the solution is obvious. The problem and solution, however, may not be obvious to anyone else. Many of the disagreements in interdisciplinary or cross-agency meetings are due to differing assumptions about the nature of a problem. For instance, suppose Joan Garcia, who has been labeled as having chronic mental illness, frequently comes to work and sits and cries. Joan, her psychiatric nurse, and a vocational rehabilitation counselor meet and discover that each has a different explanation of and solution for Joan's crying: 1) She is frustrated because the job is too hard, and she needs easier work; 2) she and her husband are not getting along, and they need couples counseling; and 3) she is getting lots of supervisor attention for crying and should get more attention for working and less for crying. If each of them presents only a preferred solution and does not explain the reason for it, then agreement is unlikely. If each person presents an explanation, then all three explanations can be analyzed by everyone involved.

8. *Make emotions explicit and legitimate.* Nearly all human services negotiations involve strong emotions because people's lives are the subject of the discussions. It would be silly to ignore those feelings, but it is not productive to let problem-solving sessions dissolve into emotional outpourings.

One unusual and effective technique to contain the impact of emotions was used in the 1950s by the Human Relations Committee, a labor-management group set up in the steel industry to handle emerging conflicts before they became serious problems. The members of the committee adopted the rule that only one person could get angry at a time. This made it legitimate for others not to respond stormily to an angry outburst. It also made letting off emotional steam easier by making an outburst itself more legitimate: "That's okay. It's his turn" (Fisher et al., 1991, p. 32).

It may be useful to establish ground rules for how to express emotions, for example, by requiring *I statements,* such as "I feel angry" and banning blaming statements such as "You made me angry." Another way to make emotions explicit and legitimate might be to periodically give participants the opportunity to express their feelings.

9. List all options first, then evaluate. Often the resolution to a problem will be a patchwork of solutions proposed by several different people. That is why it is helpful to lay out all possible options before narrowing them down. Suppose an adolescent who is on probation because he is in trouble with the law suggests as his solution dropping out of school and getting a job. His father might suggest military school, his mother might suggest counseling, and the solution ultimately agreed upon might be a combination of a special school, a part-time job, and counseling.

10. Consider multiple options. Avoid making premature judgments, and especially avoid searching for a single best answer. Such a solution does not exist. Also avoid the assumption that if one party gets more, the other party inevitably gets less.

11. Consider the consequences of the decision you suggest from the other party's perspective. Before you propose a course of action, always put yourself in the other party's shoes. For instance, one of the reasons that Jake's parents may be reluctant to bring him home is that one parent has just been laid off, and they are not sure they can feed him adequately. Or, they may be concerned about the effect his return will have on their other children. It is important that you help the parents find a solution that not only meets their son's needs but also speaks to their concerns. If you really want to find a solution, do not assume that solving the parents' dilemma is their problem. If you want to find a solution, you should make it your problem, too.

Exercise

4-7.   Suppose you are the discharge services coordinator for a prison unit for people with mental health problems. Sylvia Bronski, one of the inmates, is about to be discharged and needs services and a residence in the community. She has chronic schizophrenia that is controlled by daily medication. She is not dangerous, but she starts hallucinating and loses touch with reality when she does not take her medication regularly. You are about to meet with Ms. Bronski; a representative of a very overworked and understaffed community mental health center; and Ms. Bronski's sister, a single parent with a limited income and two preschool-age children. With three colleagues or classmates, role-play the meeting intended to establish community services for Ms. Bronski. Use the principled negotiation strategies described previously.

DIANA'S STORY CONTINUES

One month later, Diana asks, "Akram, what happened when you went back to your boss about changing the policy concerning when to put kids back in abusive homes?"

"Well, you know at first I really dreaded bringing it up again. I had been so out of control before, so upset. I guess it's harder to be calm, rational, and professional than to shoot off your mouth. I kept putting off meeting with my boss—had lots of reasons, was very busy, I told myself. In the meantime I worked on the exercises in this chapter. They are tough!"

Diana and the others in their group start agreeing how hard the chapter and exercises were. As the conversation gets louder, Hunter Greene, Diana's good friend from the apartment across the hall, knocks on the door.

When Diana opens the door, Hunter says, "Diana, what's going on? It sounds like a riot. I've noticed you have these loud, excited meetings once a month. Is this some off-the-wall cult?"

Laughing, Diana invites Hunter in and introduces the group. When everyone explains what they have been doing, Hunter, who is a physical therapist in a center for older adults, asks to stay and join the discussion. Everyone agrees, and Kathryn says "Good, someone else to help us with these exercises!"

Later, Diana remembers Akram's problem and suggests to the group, "Before you go, Akram never finished telling us what happened with his policy disagreement."

"Well, after lots of procrastination I spoke with my supervisor. I had typed up some current research findings to back up my arguments. It was a little uncomfortable at first, but she heard me out, asked some good questions, and now I'm going to head up a task force to present the issue to the agency director in a meeting in 2 months."

Someone says, "So all you got was a brush-off and more work."

"No," Akram replies, "I'm looking at it as a chance to begin to make a change in the system. Well, folks, this was really helpful, but I have to run. I still have some notes to write up tonight. See you next month at my place."

CHAPTER 5

Time Management
or
A Time for Every Purpose Under the Heaven

> *Keep in mind always the present you are constructing. It*
> *should be the future you want.*
>
> *(Walker, 1989, p. 238)*

We all have time. This chapter is about time and the human services professional. We all have things to do and time to do them in. The
challenge is to use time in ways that make us productive, effective, and
satisfied. For most human services professionals, time management is
a balancing act that involves dividing our time among service provi-
sion, paperwork, and coordination/communication with colleagues.
There is always more to do than there is time to do it in, so we have to
constantly make decisions about the best use of our time.

Exercises

Some typical time management skills are being on time for appointments, using voice mail and e-mail effectively, setting limits, managing interruptions, meeting deadlines, and managing
distractions.

5-1.   What time management skills do you have? Of those,
       which are the strongest?
5-2.   What time management skills could you improve? How
       might you make these skills more effective?

MYTHS ABOUT TIME AND TIME MANAGEMENT

There are innumerable myths about how we use time. Some of the
most common follow:

- *I haven't got time to use all that time management stuff* (Scott, 1980).
  Saying that you're too busy to think about time management is the
  perfect excuse for never taking control of your time and is just plain
  silly. If you never take a serious look at how you use time and
  whether there is anything you want to change about how you use
  it, then you have only yourself to blame.
- *The people I work with won't let me manage my time the way I want*
  (Scott, 1980). This puts the blame for your misuse of time squarely
  on other people. You cannot expect your colleagues, your boss, or
  the people you serve to magically stop interrupting, to stop coming
  up with new projects for you, or to stop calling. There are, however,
  ways to manage these problems. Some of these solutions are discussed in depth later in this chapter.

- *Time management is boring* (Scott, 1980). This can be another way to say you don't want to take responsibility for taking control of your time. An alternative perspective is thinking of time management not as an "it" but as a process composed of choices about how to use your time. You can choose interesting ways to manage your time.
- *How I manage my time is just part of my personality.* Wrong! We use time in certain ways because we have learned to do so, because there are cues in our working environments for using time in those ways, or because we are getting something out of using time in those ways. You can change how you manage time by learning new skills or by finding ways to change the cues or consequences for your use of time.
- *If I use time management, my life will be too controlled* (Scott, 1980). If you use time management deliberately, *you* will be the person in control of your time. Perhaps you equate time management with having every minute scheduled, and you value spontaneity. Time management, however, does not mean your whole life is scheduled in advance! It means routine responsibilities are scheduled and controlled, leaving you more free time to be spontaneous and creative.

STRATEGIES FOR TIME MANAGEMENT

One of the major flaws in many books and workshops on time management is that they start by giving you specific techniques for managing your time more efficiently. The technique-centered approach ignores the fact that we are all unique and may have problems with time management that require individualized solutions. You are more likely to find a solution that works for you when you use the following steps:

1. *Identify your time-use goals.* This includes what you want to do tomorrow, next week, and next month (and perhaps even further in the future). Accomplishments might include calls to be made, meetings to attend, or projects to finish.
2. *Find out whether you are currently meeting your goals.* If you are not meeting your goals, then identify what is keeping you from meeting them. Identify the barriers that get in the way of your attempts to accomplish what you set out to do.
3. *Design and use methods for solving time management problems.* For instance, you might decide just to take incoming telephone calls in the morning instead of all day long. Or, you might focus on ending interruptions quickly by saying, "This is a bad time for me right now. When can I get back to you?"
4. *Find out whether your solutions are effective.*

The remainder of this chapter is about how to use these four steps. As you work through the chapter, please remember that time management is an *ongoing* process, not a one-time activity. Every time there is a change in your work situation or job responsibilities, there is a good chance you will have to change how you manage your time. It does not mean that you have failed; it just means that circumstances have changed, so you may have to change with them.

Identifying Time-Use Goals

There are two ways of evaluating how a person uses time. One way is to evaluate *results.* This means looking at what the person has accomplished as a result of what he has done. In human services, examples of consumer-related accomplishments might include whether a youth in the juvenile justice system stays out of trouble after graduating from high school, whether a child has learned to get along with peers, whether an individual with a previous substance abuse problem has returned to work, or whether there is less violence in a family. Some other results are administrative, such as paperwork that is up-to-date, development of a new assessment tool, or a completed order for the month's food supply for a consumer's home.

The second way to evaluate your time use is to look at the *process* of what you do. In other words, look at how time is spent. Typical ways we spend time in human services include meeting with consumers of services, meeting with people from other agencies, and meeting in informal brainstorming sessions with colleagues.

When you identify your time-use and accomplishment goals, you need to consider what you want to do and what you have to do (i.e., what is required of you). It is important to consider both "want to's" and "have to's" because they are seldom identical (though they often overlap). If we combine them with time-use goals and accomplishment goals, we come up with the following four questions:

1. Am I currently achieving the results I want to achieve?
2. Am I currently achieving the results I am expected to achieve?
3. How do I want to spend my professional time?
4. How do I have to spend my professional time?

Exercise

5-3. It is often useful to identify goals for managing various periods of time.
     a. If you are currently working in human services, then create a chart for yourself similar to the one shown in Figure 1.

b. If you are a student and are not currently working in human services, then try creating two different charts similar to the one shown in Figure 1. First, create one for yourself in your role as a student. Second, find someone currently working in the human services field that you have chosen, and ask her or him to fill out the chart and talk about it with you.

Another way to view your professional activities is to divide them into high-payoff activities (HIPOs) and low-payoff activities (LOPOs). HIPOs, such as long-term planning, building working relationships, long-term development of a new funding source, or establishment of a

	Results		
	Next month	Next week	Tomorrow
I want my professional activities to result in . . .	Ongoing communication with local mental health agencies	Starting to find a speech-language therapist	Preparing material for upcoming core meetings
	Better communication with the department	Beginning to write proposal to obtain funding sources for wheelchair	Gathering data for month-end reports
My professional activities must result in . . .	Getting funding for wheelchair repairs	Completing month-end reports	Answering two letters from parents
	Contracting services of a speech-language therapist	Attending two core meetings	Scheduling meeting on client issues
			Returning telephone calls

	Process		
	Next month	Next week	Tomorrow
I want to spend my professional time . . .	Reading related journal articles	Developing plans for in-service training for department	Gathering ideas to present to my supervisor
	Attending professional conferences or seminars	Discussing long-range plans with my supervisor	Calling charitable organizations for donations
I must spend my professional time. . .	Finding alternative funding sources	Attending meetings	Being in office 8 hours
	Preparing for state inspection	Meeting other requests on time	Responding to telephone calls and drop-ins

Figure 1. Time management self-assessment.

new treatment program, are building blocks that lead to major accomplishments. HIPOs are important, but they can take time to accomplish and often are not well-defined. LOPOs are often specific tasks that are easy to do and make you feel as though you have accomplished something. LOPOs, however, may not make much difference in the long run ("Review of *Just in Time*," 1986).

Exercise

5-4. Evaluate your work or school activities using the HIPO/ LOPO model.
   a. If you are currently working in human services, then list five common professional HIPOs and five common LOPOs.
   b. If you are a student, then list five common school-related HIPOs and five common LOPOs.

Assessing Current Time Use

You will not know whether you are meeting your goals for use of your professional time unless you know how you are currently using your time and whether you are currently achieving what you want to achieve. One way to assess your current use of time is by keeping a time log similar to the one shown in Figure 2, which shows Bill Martinez' time log for 1 work day. Bill is a counselor in a program for unemployed veterans.

Exercises

5-5. Keep a time log for a week (or for as long as you can, if a week is too long), using a chart similar to the one shown in Figure 2. Under "Cues" and "Consequences," include anything you think might be related to how you use your time.
5-6. Now look at your answers to the chart you completed for Exercise 5-3 about how you *want* to spend your time and how you *must* spend your time. Compare those answers with how you really spent your time as shown on your time log. Did you meet your goals?
5-7. Finally, look at your answers to the chart you completed for Exercise 5-3 about what results you want to achieve and what results you are required to achieve in the next week. Compare these answers with what you actually accomplished during the week you completed the time log. Did you meet your time goals?

Time Log

Date	Time	Cues	How I Reacted	Consequences
7/10	8:20 A.M.	Smell of coffee	Chatted with Jan and Mark	Avoided telephone messages
	9:30 A.M.		Made calls	Got stiff from sitting
	10:45 A.M.	Heard mail delivery	Got mail, wrote letters	Moved around, felt better
	11:30 A.M.	Hunger!	Met client for lunch appt.	Felt good: helped client solve a problem
	1:00 P.M.		Went to staff meeting	Learned about new meeting technique
	2:00–5:00 P.M.		Conducted one group and two individual sessions	Tired! Two sessions went well, one didn't.

Figure 2.   Time log for Bill Martinez.

Heidi Daly

You never have enough time. I could have probably put in 60, 70 hours a week at the nursing home, and I still wouldn't get everything done because there's always something. But I made sure that I limited the amount of time that I spent at the nursing home because it would have made it more stressful to not have the time to get away, doing something that is totally opposite, just relaxing. You can't do that when you're still working, even when you bring work home. I would bring work home, and then I'd be stressed out because I wasn't doing it. So, I tried to limit bringing work home and told myself I would not work more than 45 or 50 hours a week. It did cut into some of the things that I needed to do, but I couldn't be the best person, the best worker, if I put more time in. I could give myself more constructively if I lessened the amount of time.

Christa Pavlus

I've really learned that setting a schedule with my patients has helped me with my time management a lot. We used to just have our caseload, and we'd just go see somebody, whoever we thought might be available. [Scheduling is] the best way to communicate with all the other disciplines so that they know what we're doing, and when we're doing it. That way we can plan out when I need to see these people. That way I don't come to the end of the day and go, "Oh my gosh, I still have to see these two people."

Johnn Young

I'm forever taking time management courses. I think I'm getting to be the guru of time management courses. I do a lot of time management because I realize when things get discombobulated, I have to go back and say, "Okay, what's important to me, what do I need to get done?" Then I have to go back and refocus. Just getting to the bathroom, sometimes I have to schedule it, because I would go through my whole day, do all the work I have to do, and then at the end of it realize I have not taken care of me.

On the corner of my desk I have an hourglass. I've finally gotten my office to be kind of inviting, and people will come and just sit. They don't want anything, they'll just come and sit. One day I was in here working, and in half an hour there were five people in my office. I had to leave my office to go do my work. I'll turn the hourglass over and say "You have until this glass is empty to leave (it runs about 20 minutes)," and so far it works. Somebody turned it over on its side, and I said, "Okay, now you have to leave."

Time management definitely is a biggie and something that I think I will be working on the rest of my life. I just will.

Analyzing Time-Use Problems

There are three general causes of time-use problems. The first type of problem occurs 1) when you are easily distracted into wasting time or 2) when you spend too much time on work that is urgent but unimportant (Covey, 1989). Distractions include following the smell of freshly brewed coffee into the breakroom or chatting with a colleague who often drops by to gossip. Examples of urgent but unimportant work vary with the situation but usually include some meetings and interruptions or tasks that someone else has labeled important or emergencies when in fact they are not.

A second cause of time-use problems is when you do not have all the skills you need to manage time effectively. Examples of skills needed to manage time are

- Chairing a meeting in a way that gives everyone the chance to contribute but gives no one the chance to monopolize

- Gracefully ending a conversation with someone who wants to keep talking with you
- Managing telephone interruptions
- Knowing how to say no when you already have too much to do
- Setting up a daily "to do" list and working through it
- Using a computer effectively

The third type of cause is either when there are not enough positive consequences for using your time in a way that meets your goals or when you are getting too many rewards for using your time ineffectively. Such rewards can keep you from using time well because they can reinforce your time mismanagement. Following are examples of these rewards.

Attention Some people get attention by playing the martyr and telling others how hard they work ("Oh, how overworked I am!"). Others continue to arrive late for meetings because they get to be the center of attention, particularly when they rush in breathless and apologetically say they were managing a crisis (Scott, 1980).

Power Most of us have been at meetings in which one of the people whose presence is needed arrives 15 minutes late. When a person's input is needed before arriving at a group decision, showing up late places that person in a powerful position (Scott, 1980).

Avoidance of Tasks When we procrastinate and put off unpleasant tasks, we often do so with the hope that if we delay long enough, then someone else will do our work for us. Also, sometimes we put off boring or unpleasant tasks because it is more fun to "brainstorm" with colleagues (the solution to this habit is to reward yourself for finishing that boring report by spending time doing more enjoyable professional activities) (Scott, 1980).

Resistance to Change Change is hard for most people. It can be very difficult to give up old, familiar ways of managing time even when new tactics will be more effective (Scott, 1980). (See Chapter 8 for a discussion of the effects of change.)

Avoidance of Responsibility When you hear someone say "Why didn't you remind me those reports were due yesterday?" you are hearing one of the people who avoid taking responsibility for their own actions (Scott, 1980).

Excitement and Stimulation Some people need more excitement in their lives than others. If they have not found functional ways to get that excitement, then they may mismanage their time to get more stimulation. Individuals who always run in breathlessly at the last minute or who always meet deadlines with seconds to spare may be filling their personal excitement quota (Scott, 1980).

Exercise

5-8. Use the information you have from Exercises 5-1 through 5-7 to decide whether your approach to time management needs any improvement. If so, then analyze your current use of time and decide

  a. Whether you want to change any cues for time use

  b. Whether you want to learn any new time management skills

  c. Whether you want to change the consequences you receive for your time use

Designing and Using Time Management Solutions

After you have identified your time-use goals; assessed any ways you are not meeting these goals; and pinpointed your problems with cues, skills, and/or consequences that may need to be solved, it is time to pick a solution. Following are several typical ways to improve how you manage your professional time (see Chapter 8 for a discussion of personal time). Remember, however, these techniques may not work for everyone. Use your creativity to pick time management strategies that will work for you!

Cues for Time Management Sometimes cues make it easy to waste time, sometimes they are helpful, and sometimes we need to create new ones. Sometimes it is difficult to manage your time effectively because it is not clear what you are supposed to be doing. A common starting place for improving time management is to ask for clarification about your responsibilities, how they differ from other people's responsibilities, and what you are expected to achieve (Maher & Cook, 1985). If you ask for a specific job description and do not get one, then you may want to write one and ask your supervisor to approve it.

Sometimes we do not have good ways of remembering what we need to do. It is amazing how many people expect to be able to remember all of the things they are supposed to do without writing them down. Unless you are the rare individual who has a photographic memory, lists are important time management tools. Most of us are familiar with the daily "to do" list. "To do" lists are often divided into three categories: things to do, calls to make, and people to see. It also helps to have paper and pencil with you throughout the day so you can make lists of tasks as they occur to you. In the middle of a meeting, for instance, you may suddenly remember that you need to call Ms. Lacaille. Or, during a telephone conversation you may remember a letter you promised to write for Mr. Malik. If you have something to write with and something to write on, then you can capture those tasks on paper.

Another common barrier to effective time management may be found in poor scheduling. If this is a problem for you, then consider the calendar you use. As with other techniques, no one calendar works for everyone. Experiment until you find one that is right for you. Then, when you schedule time, be sure that you do the following:

1. Reserve enough time for each activity (including time for travel with some extra for traffic jams and road construction).
2. Match the task to the time of day and your energy level (e.g., if you do your best paperwork in the morning, hold all calls between 8 A.M. and 9 A.M.).
3. Match the activity to the people and resources you need to complete the activity (e.g., make sure the people you need to consult on that special project are available at the times you want to consult them).
4. Divide big projects into small, manageable steps, and set deadlines for completing each step (Mayer, 1995).
5. Finally, do not forget to make appointments with yourself. Time you need alone to think about projects or to write reports is just as important as time spent in meetings and appointments that involve other people. In addition, include in your calendar some way to remind yourself of routine responsibilities or follow-up calls you need to complete. This type of reminder is often called a *tickler file*.

One of the most important tools used in human services is the telephone. Unfortunately, it is also one of the biggest barriers to effective time management. If it is possible, do have calls held if you are in a meeting (including meetings with yourself), and do have calls screened so that you can pull out any notes you need or otherwise prepare for the call. Some people set up regular times they make outgoing calls and accept incoming calls every day so that they can do most of their telephone work in one time period (Maher & Cook, 1985). If your position requires you to accept all incoming calls, you can still provide cues for people to call at certain times. For instance, you might tell callers, "The best time to reach me is before noon," or, "I'm usually easier to reach if you call on Monday, Wednesday, or Thursday." Also, if you are interrupted by a call while you are in the middle of a project, then you can say, for example, "I'm in the middle of something else right now. May I get back to you in an hour?" One indispensable aid to effective use of the telephone is a list of frequently used telephone numbers. Some people prefer to use address books (written or electronic), speed-dialing functions, files of business cards, or some other system. Again, use whatever works for you.

If you have e-mail, it can be a time saver when you leave clear, detailed messages that would be too complex to leave on voice mail. As with making telephone calls, develop a strategy for using e-mail (e.g., dealing with it once daily) that works for you.

Your filing system can also be an obstacle to efficient time management. No one filing system works for everyone. Consider what papers you will need often and set up a system that makes it easy for you to find and retrieve those papers.

Waiting is something we all do, often unexpectedly. We wait for meetings to start, for cars to be repaired, for appointments with health care providers. We often think of waiting time as lost time, but it can be a cue to clear away some work-related tasks. Sometimes it is possible to call ahead and find out whether there will be a wait. More often, delays cannot be predicted. Waiting time can be productive time if you always have short tasks or reading with you. Some of the author's most productive professional time has been spent in car repair shop waiting rooms because no one can call her there!

Suzanne Cardiff

You have to pace yourself, and you have to manage your time. The biggest thing I see, especially in case workers, is they go a million miles an hour trying to get everything done until they burn out. That's not time management. You've gotta learn to pace yourself throughout the day. You can't always get everything done, so you have to learn to pace yourself according to what you can handle. On some days you may need to go in to work 12 hours, but the next day you work 6. You've gotta balance it out.

Pamela Meister

Time management is an issue because we are in a situation with two of us as patient representatives, and we only have one computer. Because of budget cutbacks they won't give us another computer, so we have three systems on one computer with two of us dealing with patient complaints. Fortunately Ann [the other patient representative] and I get along so well that we're very respectful of each other's time, and we can really work with each other.

Time Management Skills   As noted previously, time management is a set of skills, not a fixed part of your personality.

Time Alone   One of the hardest skills to learn is doing just one thing at a time. Because there is always too much to do in human services, as you work on one task three other important tasks will occur to you. A useful way to cope when this happens is to make a note of the other tasks but not interrupt your original work to do them (Maher & Cook, 1985). Another common problem is having many different things to do and being undecided about where to begin. A possible solution to this problem is to give every job a due date. Then you can pick what to do based on when you want to have it done. A deadline does not have to be imposed on you from the outside: It can be your decision about when you want to complete a job. Another approach some people find useful is to do part of one project, then move on to part of another project, and so forth. This tactic increases variety, but it may not be for you if you like to concentrate on one project for an extended period of time.

Another useful way to manage time working alone is to group similar tasks together. For instance, you might make all the telephone calls on your "to do" list in 1 hour, deal with all your correspondence in half an hour, and so forth. Also, when you schedule a large block of time to do desk work, it helps to get up to walk around and stretch every so often. No one can concentrate on one task indefinitely, so it helps to give yourself a break and some variety.

Interruptions   It is not always possible to avoid interruptions by having calls held or by closing your office door. In that case, skills at managing interruptions become important. Most people are receptive when you diplomatically tell them that you are in the middle of a project and then ask them when you can get back to them. This may not, however, be a comfortable tactic when the person interrupting you is your supervisor. An interruption from a supervisor can often be handled effectively with a response such as "I'm about halfway done with the report you asked me to complete by this afternoon. Would you prefer that I put the report on hold for the moment, or shall I get back to you on this new issue later?" This approach lets your supervisor know what you are doing and takes the choice about whether to continue the interruption out of your hands.

Meetings   Most meetings can be improved by time limits, set agendas, attendance by necessary people only, and prompt beginnings and endings. If you are not clear about the purpose of a meeting, then ask! If you are not clear about what you are expected to contribute, then ask! If you are chairing a meeting, then it is your responsibility to clarify the purpose of the meeting and the contributions expected from all participants. Also, it is your responsibility to begin and end the meeting on time and, in a longer meeting, to begin and end breaks on time (Mayer, 1995).

Doing It Anyway   Sometimes a job has to be done right away, and you do not want to do it right away. If there is no escape, then the only solution is to grit your teeth and do the task anyway. You may not enjoy yourself while you are doing it, but you can reward yourself for getting the job done.

Learning to Say No   The better you are at your job, the more likely people are to ask you to do more work. In addition, human services agencies never have enough money, so there is always more work to do than there are people to do it. It is helpful to remember that if you try to do too much, then you will not do anything very well. One graceful way to say no to additional work is to explain, "I'm very flattered that you asked, but I'm so busy already that if I said yes, then I would not be able to do it as well as both of us would want the job done." The emphasis on downsizing and cost containment can make people reluctant to say no because they are afraid of losing their jobs. This can be a trap: If you never say no, then you will probably find yourself trying to do far more than is humanly possible. All of us do sometimes say yes to work that we would rather not do, but no one can do it all.

Give Yourself Positive Consequences for Effective Time Management   A common cause of numerous time management problems is to say, "I'll do this task that I enjoy first and save the unpleasant one for later." This approach sets you up for failure. You end up punishing yourself (because you must do a job you do not enjoy) for doing something you find pleasant. A more successful strategy is to give yourself the opportunity to do something you like as a reward for completing an unpleasant chore. For instance, you might reward yourself for making a difficult telephone call by having a brainstorming session with a favorite co-worker.

Another way to reward yourself for using time effectively is to put up a chart, graph, or sign in your office that shows how much you have accomplished. You can post any type of information you choose: Number of calls made, number of reports completed, and amount of time spent providing direct services are examples of information human services professionals have posted.

Exercise

5-9.   Design a plan to improve your time management, and use it for a week or a month, depending on the nature of the plan.

Evaluating Time-Use Interventions

No time management tactic is worth using unless it helps you achieve your goals. Once you start using a new approach to improving how you manage time, use it long enough to give it a fair trial. If your new approach is something you will use daily, then give it at least a week or two. If your new approach is something you use weekly, then try it for at least a month. Then decide whether your new approach is a success. Following are four good questions to ask as you decide:

1. Did you meet your goal?
2. If you met your goal, was your new tactic responsible for your success?
3. Did any unintended effects (good or bad) result from your new tactic?
4. How do you feel about what you have done and the results you have achieved?   (adapted from Maher & Cook, 1985)

If you decide your tactic is a success, then all you have to do is to keep using it. If it is not successful, then modify it or drop it, and try a different approach. Remember that this evaluation process is an essential part of having good time management skills.

Exercises

5-10.   Evaluate the plan for improving your time management that you designed in Exercise 5-9.
5-11.   Use your time management skills to remind yourself to come back to this exercise 1 month after you finish this chapter. When that time comes, go back and answer Exercise 5-1 again. Have your answers changed at all during the month? Have your time management skills improved?
5-12.   Pick a friend or colleague who seems to get a lot done, and shadow that person for a day, or interview him or her about how he or she manages professional time.

TIME FOR DIANA

Diana and her friends have been working on the first few exercises in Chapter 5. At their next regular meeting, Hunter says, "Have these been an eye-opener! I've been spending way too much time putting out fires and not nearly enough on long-term projects. I've got to figure out a way to change that."

Diana reports, "My problem is that my supervisor keeps adding to the list of what I'm supposed to be doing, and I have to figure out either how to manage my time better or how to get better at setting limits so I don't work 60 hours a week. It's probably some of both."

"It's a good thing we've set a time for ending the business part of these gatherings," Akram chimes in. "It's time to stop working and bring out the food." No one disagrees.

CHAPTER 6

Communication

or

Did You Say What I Heard?

OBJECTIVES

- Describe guidelines for effective communication, and learn how to use them.

- Develop a plan for working with difficult individuals.

When the use of language results, as it so often does, in the
creation or aggravation of disagreements and conflict,
there is something linguistically wrong with the speaker,
the listener, or both.

(Hayakawa et al., 1991, p. 12)

The world runs on communication. Life as we know it simply
would not exist if we could not communicate with one another. Communication is perhaps more important in human services than in other
professions, for all of our professional relationships are based on communication. Everyday life is also extraordinarily complex, with endless
possibilities for effective or ineffective communication. This chapter is
designed to provide the reader with basic guidelines for effective communication and for working with difficult people. Although the strategies described in this chapter are useful with both professionals and
consumers of services, the focus here is on communication with colleagues. Communication with human services consumers is obviously
of great importance, and there are numerous sources of education
about effective communication with those we serve. In the author's
opinion, there unfortunately is too little education available about communication with colleagues. Therefore, that topic is the focus of this
chapter.

William Esp

Communication: With clinical staff I don't have a problem. With administrative staff there is always a huge problem.
There's decisions I believe they make based on numbers without
really consulting the people that are in the trenches. It is so hard
communicating what you know works. A lot of times, you don't
have empirical evidence of it. You know in your heart that it
works and it's effective and it's crucial to your program. Administrators are wanting to cut it because they're saying, "Well we
have no data that says that this works."

My guess is that they probably have the same frustration with
me in terms of getting me to understand their language. A lot of
times it's like oil and water, and it's always been the biggest
struggle for me, not acting out. I know I have an anti-authority
kind of character, and I can get those buttons pushed real easy.
I've learned how to balance that, and I've been there for 6 years.
Though people have been probably frustrated with me and me
with them, I think I've been able to maintain a respectful
relationship.

Johnn Young

Some of the work I do comes out of the gay men's community, some of the work I do comes out of the non-gay African American community. Even if you speak one language, you have to be bilingual. There's certain things that are not okay to say in the African American community, there's definitely some things you can't say in the gay community, and there's some things you can't say in the African American gay community. For example, *queer* is getting to be very big in the young gay community. In the African American community, if you refer to someone as being queer, you have just insulted them. In the African American gay community, that's not our struggle, that's not what we're after—we're after reclaiming our own self-esteem and our place.

GUIDELINES FOR EFFECTIVE COMMUNICATION

Effective communication requires a focus on the interaction between the people involved. Here are guidelines for making communication effective.

Listen Carefully

Listen carefully is the most frequently stated and most frequently broken rule for good communication. That is unfortunate, for we learn far more by listening than by talking (Mayer, 1995). Careful, active listening requires all of one's attention, and it is much more difficult to listen well than to talk well. Active listening includes paying careful attention to verbal and nonverbal cues. It is very different from the kind of listening most of us do in ordinary conversation, when we may daydream or let our minds wander. The most common obstacle to careful listening is failing to pay enough attention to the speaker. Too often, when conversing with others, we are not really paying attention: We are merely planning our responses and waiting until it is our turn to talk, or we are daydreaming.

Have you ever been talking with someone and realized that what you heard is not what she or he said? Here is an example of this type of failure in listening skills: Your supervisor says she wants the proposal you are working on completed by the end of the week and that she wants to be kept informed of your progress. You start thinking about what you need to do to finish in time and do not pay careful attention to the rest of her comments. The next day she comes into your office at 11:00 A.M. and is irate because you did not follow her instruction to fill her in by 9:00 each morning!

Two tactics will help prevent your misunderstanding what has been said to you. One tactic is *paraphrasing* (Giampa, Walker-Burt, & Lamb, 1984). When you paraphrase, you test how well you understood what you heard by putting the other person's ideas in your own words. For instance, suppose Mark, one of your colleagues, says to you, "Sondra is so flaky, I can't count on her for anything." This is a rather general statement that could refer to any number of problems. To find out whether your colleague means what you think he means, you might ask him, "Do you mean that she is almost always late to meetings?" If your colleague replies, "Yes," then your paraphrase has helped you find out that you heard what he said correctly.

Suppose, however, that your colleague replies, "No, she's usually on time for meetings, but she doesn't seem well-prepared for them. I don't think she does her homework." You discover not only that your first interpretation was incorrect but also what your colleague meant. Now, suppose instead that your colleague replies, "No, she's usually on time. She's just flaky, you know what I mean." At this point, the odds are good that you do *not* know what he means. To find out, you might try being direct and asking a question such as "Can you give me an example of something she's done recently that you consider flaky?"

Another useful tactic for the active listener is *perception checking* (Giampa et al., 1984). Perception checking is usually used to find out whether the other person is feeling what you think the person is feeling. For instance, if you think a colleague is upset, then you might say, "I get the sense that you're angry with me right now. Is that true?" Or, you might say, "It sounds to me like you're pretty unhappy with the way things are. Is that right?" Of course, if you ask questions such as these, then you must be willing to hear the answers. When you ask whether a person is angry, the response may be "You bet I'm angry, you so-and-so, and here's why . . ." In the author's opinion, however, it is better to know what is going on than to ignore subtle signals or misread a situation completely. Furthermore, it is most helpful to check your perceptions as soon as possible after you identify the need to do so. If you wait to check and act on an incorrect perception, you may create an unnecessary problem.

Attend to Nonverbal as Well as Verbal Communication

Language is just one of the tools we use to communicate. Nonverbal communication tools also are extremely important. Here is a partial list of nonverbal tools that are used in communication: eyes, hands, handshake, stance, walk, tone of voice, head, face, smile, posture, use of touch, nervous mannerisms such as foot swinging or tapping a pencil, vocal intensity, and vocal volume (Axtell, 1991; Dima, 1990). There are books available that claim to tell you what various nonverbal forms of communication mean. Beware of them! Interpretations of nonverbal signals are culturally based (Axtell, 1991; Dima, 1990). Thus, the same signal can have two completely different meanings in two different cultures. In some cultures, for instance, shaking the head up and down means *no*, a signal likely to confuse someone from the United States where the same signal means *yes*. Similarly, signals can also have different meanings in different parts of a single country. Another caution is to avoid attributing too much meaning to certain nonverbal behavior. For instance, a person's fidgeting may mean that person is uncomfortable with what you are saying, or it could just as easily mean that the available seating is physically uncomfortable, that the meeting has lasted too long, or that the individual has a medical condition of which restlessness or shakiness is a symptom. Some of us are less able to sit still for long meetings than others.

It is important to be as aware of the nonverbal signals you are giving as you are of those you are receiving. For instance, do you look down at papers on the table when you are uninterested or uncomfortable with what the speaker has to say? Do you avoid eye contact with someone who is expressing anger with you? Avoiding eye contact can be a mistake because doing so may be seen as evidence that you are not listening. Eye contact may be difficult to provide in these instances, however, because one's first impulse is usually not to look at someone who is yelling at us. Do you turn away when you disagree with a speaker? When you are physically uncomfortable, can the ways you show that discomfort be misread as lack of attention or agreement?

Johnn Young

When it comes to communicating with people, there are so many different styles, and some of them are culturally based. Everybody wants the same things: Everybody wants to be heard, they want to be appreciated, they want to be cared for, they want to know that they're important, but how they do that is so different. With the African American gay men's group, people will sit and tell their stories and their impressions. [In] some of the other gay groups, people will tell their stories, but they'll also talk about their solutions. In [the African American group] people sit and think, "Well there's nothing I can do." My place in that group is saying, "Well, let's think about the possibilities, maybe there's something you can do. Maybe you can go in there and have a different attitude and think, 'Okay, my boss is pushing me. Obviously he thinks I have more potential than I do, and I'm going to live up to that,' instead of thinking, 'okay, my boss is pushing me, he must be against me.' " So different communication styles are real interesting in this work. It creates a challenge.

Talk so that People Will Listen

People listen when the speaker is saying something important or useful to them; when the speaker is someone they like, respect, and/or find interesting; and when the speaker speaks well (Hamlin, 1989). Whenever you find yourself listening intently to someone, ask yourself what that person is doing to hold your attention and how you might learn to do the same.

Use Language to Foster Cooperation, Not Argument

The language we use shapes how we think and how we interact with others. If we provide critiques, engage in debates, consider others' statements controversial and provocative, and focus on differences, we are likely to see the world in two-sided, win-lose terms. If we offer comments, invite and engage in discussions, consider others' statements to be important and thought-provoking, and focus on the search for common ground, we are likely to see the world in multiple points of view, win-win terms (Tannen, 1998).

Be Sensitive to the Emotional Content of Language

Two words with essentially the same dictionary meaning can have vastly different emotional content. Thus, you can create or defuse emotional situations through the use of language, and you can identify the emotional tone set by others by attending to the emotional content of their language. For instance, consider the following descriptions given by two staff members at halfway houses regarding a client whom they have just seen jointly:

Stan: Boy, was that last fellow defensive! Uptight and not willing to admit to half the problems in his life. He's going to be difficult to counsel effectively.

Marcia: Stan, we have very different perceptions of our client. He struck me as reserved and was very clear about what he wanted to discuss and what he did not want to discuss. I think he's set some well-defined limits that I found very reasonable.

Both staff members agreed that the man they saw held some of his emotions back, but they labeled and evaluated that action very differently. The first staff member used the negatively weighted words *up-*

tight and *defensive*, whereas the second described the same approach as *reserved*.

Exercises

6-1.   For the next three meetings or classes you attend, pay careful attention to and make notes concerning the non-verbal signals that you and others give. Also note whether the people you observe are responding more to verbal or nonverbal signals when the two are not conveying the same message.

6-2.   Categorize each word listed below in terms of its emotional value for you. Indicate whether you feel each to be positive, negative, or neutral.

Conservative   Masculine
Liberal   Feminine
Sensitive   Discreet
Defensive   Private
Cheerful   Depressed
Needy   Manipulative
Strong

6-3.   For 1 day, carry a file card or a piece of paper and pencil with you and list every word you hear to which you have a strong emotional reaction, whether it is positive or negative.

Remember the Difference Between Language and Reality

A map is not the territory it stands for; words are not things. A map does not represent all of a territory; words never say all about anything. The meanings of words are not in the words; they are in us. Beware of definitions, which are words about words. Think with examples rather than definitions whenever possible.

(Hayakawa, 1964, pp. 314–315)

Many of the words we use to describe how people act are summary words: They are a personal shorthand for a number of specific behaviors. The previous example using the word *flaky* illustrates use of such a summary word. Probably the most common and misused summary word the author knows is *inappropriate*. *Never,* when told someone is acting in a way that is *inappropriate,* assume you know specifically what the speaker means! *Inappropriate* can mean everything from "She wears pants, and I think she should be wearing a skirt" to "He exposes his genitals in public," with a host of other interpretations in between. That is why Hayakawa's recommendation to think with examples is so important. If you think with examples and use paraphrasing, your ability to understand what other speakers are saying will be much greater than if you simply assume you know what others are talking about.

Beware of Jargon

Professional jargon is usually a collection of specialized terms and acronyms, a form of verbal shorthand. When jargon is used outside of groups of people who understand it, it inevitably makes communication less effective. Human services workers occasionally use jargon or abbreviations, and they often are so accustomed to these terms that they forget others do not understand. Sometimes jargon is used to control a situation by keeping others ignorant. If a colleague with whom you are speaking sprinkles conversations with jargon that you do not understand, then *ask* what the speaker means. To reduce your own use of jargon, you may want to keep a list of acronyms and terms to avoid so that people who use your services and/or colleagues in other agencies will know what you are talking about. Reducing your use of jargon will be useful because service consumers often feel too intimidated to ask for clarification of such terms.

Jargon that interferes with communication is not limited to human services. When the author moved to Denver, she used a city map to figure out how to get around. On the map, there were two major interstate highways, I-25 going north and south and I-70 going east and west. Newscasters on local radio stations kept referring to traffic conditions on the "Valley Highway," but the author could not find the Valley Highway on the map. It took several months before she figured out that the Valley Highway was the same as I-25!

Say Only What You Are Willing to Have Repeated

When you have just finished a frustrating meeting with someone from another agency, resist the urge to go to the staff lounge and announce, "That so-and-so from XYZ agency is a real jerk!" Such an announcement should be avoided because chances are good you will have future contact with "that so-and-so." Chances are also good that someone who hears you will repeat your comment to an employee of the agency across the street, who will repeat it to the subject of your comment. Also, people who hear you say something negative about an absent colleague will wonder what you say about them when they are not around. In addition to being unsafe, nasty remarks about colleagues are very unprofessional and are unlikely to improve anyone's impression of you.

Use Feedback Effectively

Effective feedback has several characteristics:

1. *It is proactive.* Effective feedback focuses on what you want the person to *do,* not on what you want the person to stop doing. Taking a proactive approach improves the likelihood of a positive future relationship with the person receiving feedback. It also improves the likelihood that the person receiving feedback will change or consider changing in the manner you suggest. Following are two examples of proactive feedback:

   - "Stevie, I really appreciate the way you helped me with the Evans family this morning. Your knowledge of a different solution helped everyone get what they wanted. I hope you'll let me call on you for that kind of help again."

   - "Lisa, I appreciate your willingness to chair the meeting this morning. However, when you said, 'We all know what the problem is, let's find a solution,' I felt frustrated and cut off because I'm not sure I agree with your identification of the problem. When this sort of thing comes up in the future, could you ask for other people's views on the nature of the problem before moving on?"

     In the first example, the person receiving feedback found out what the speaker wanted her to keep doing. The speaker in the second example started with a positive statement and then described to Lisa what she could do differently.

2. *It is specific.* Effective feedback tells the person what was done well and/or what needs to change.

3. *It separates what the person did from its emotional effect on you.* Instead of saying, "You made me very angry this morning," say, "When you told me not to get involved in your project, I felt very angry." As in this example, effective feedback uses the word *I* to describe the speaker's emotions.

4. *It is about behavior or conditions the listener is able to change.* There is no point in giving constructive criticism about a law passed by Congress that the listener is responsible for implementing but cannot change.

5. *It is well-timed.* On the one hand, feedback that is given as soon as possible after the incident occurs makes it easy for the listener to remember the events to which the speaker is referring. On the other hand, when you have just had a very emotionally charged meeting, you may want to wait until everyone has had a chance to calm down before offering any constructive criticism.

6. *It includes a clarity check.* When you give feedback, try to make sure that the listener hears what you say. One way to accomplish this goal is to ask the listener, as diplomatically as possible, to repeat (paraphrase) what he has heard you say.

(adapted from Giampa et al., 1984)

It is often difficult to give effective feedback, especially constructive criticism. One way to make giving feedback easier is to start small; another way is to practice giving purely positive feedback first, so that you can become comfortable with it. Then, start giving small corrections to nonthreatening people and build up gradually.

Face Your Fears

Sometimes we do not communicate clearly because we are afraid of what we imagine to be the possible results. Some commonly feared situations are failing to meet expectations, offending or hurting others, being rejected, being wrong, and being unable to express oneself accurately. In some situations, those fears may be realistic; in other situations, they may not. Either way, communicating poorly will not improve relationships. It may delay whatever consequences, good or bad, that will result. Furthermore, the delay will probably cause new problems because people become frustrated when they cannot understand what someone else is saying.

If You Have Just Reached
an Important Agreement, Then Write It Down!

Putting an important agreement in writing serves two purposes. First, it serves as a final check to make sure everyone understood what was discussed and agrees to the same conditions. This prevents misunderstandings. For example, in a meeting with Mr. Black from Generic Services Inc., Mr. Black says, "Joe MacDonald needs social skills training." You say, "Yes, I agree." At the end of your meeting, some 30 minutes later, Mr. Black says, "Now, you're going to provide Mr. MacDonald with social skills training, and I'll provide the other services we've discussed." You can respond to clarify what was actually agreed on: "No, I didn't agree to provide that service; I just agreed it was needed."

The second advantage of putting agreements in writing is that it prevents faulty memory from interfering with the implementation of the agreement at a later date. Most of us have been at parties where we have played Telephone. In this game, one person whispers a statement to a second person, who then whispers it to a third person, and so on, until everyone in the room has heard it. The final person to hear the message repeats it out loud. Invariably, what the final person says and what the first person said are very different.

Ask for Help

No one has perfect communication skills. Furthermore, other people may be reluctant to give you feedback about your communication skills. It helps to be willing to ask for feedback or for specific advice on how to improve your skills. For instance, at the end of a difficult meeting, you might approach someone who also attended the meeting and whose judgment you trust and ask whether your points came across clearly.

Human services work requires interaction with a variety of professions and people. If you are unsure about how to communicate effectively with members of another profession, ask them for assistance! One useful approach is to ask "What questions should I be asking you?" (Warschaw, 1980). Another is to ask what information the person would find helpful to receive from you.

A good rule of thumb to remember is that it is usually acceptable to make a mistake once, but it is not acceptable to keep making the same mistake over and over. That is why it is better to ask for help than to flounder.

Exercises

6-4.   For 1 day, pay careful attention to how people communicate at work and/or at school. Try to identify at least one example of each of the following:
   a. **Careful listening**
       Attention to nonverbal cues
       Sensitivity to emotional content
       Recognition of the difference between language and reality
       Effective use of feedback
   b. **Poor listening**
       Failure to attend to nonverbal cues
       Insensitivity to emotional content
       Failure to recognize the difference between language and reality
       Jargon that obscures meaning
       Gossip
       Ineffective use of feedback
   c. **Defensiveness**

6-5.   For each of the examples of poor listening you found in Exercise 6-4, describe how the speaker could have communicated more effectively.

6-6.   List the 10 jargon words or phrases most frequently used at your agency or office. Translate each of those words or phrases into everyday language that can be easily understood by an individual totally unfamiliar with human services.

ELECTRONIC COMMUNICATION

Changes in modern technology inevitably affect our working lives, including how we communicate with others. The most prevalent forms of communication with colleagues and consumers of our services are the telephone, voice mail, and e-mail.

Using the Telephone

Live telephone conversations are often the lifeblood of our work. They keep us connected to the people we serve and to other professionals. Because we cannot see each other's facial expressions or body language when we communicate on the telephone, words and vocal inflection become much more important than they are in face-to-face communication. Your feelings come across in your tone of voice. If you want to convey a positive feeling, smile while you talk on the telephone. You'll sound more open, and people will more likely to warm up to you (Mayer, 1995). Pay careful attention to how the other person sounds, and when you think she or he sounds puzzled or negative, check it out.

Using Voice Mail

How did we ever live before voice mail? We can set appointments, exchange information, even agree on a plan to deliver a service without ever talking with someone directly. Lack of access to body language and facial expressions requires even more attention when you leave a message on voice mail than when you interact with someone on the telephone. Be clear about what you want to say (you may want to make a list of points to cover) and the feeling you want to convey before you pick up the telephone. Also remember that voice mail messages probably are not confidential and may well be heard by people other than the intended recipient. Many voice mail systems allow you to re-record your message. If you do not like what you said or how you sounded the first time you left your message, then use the re-record feature, and do it again! It's worth taking a few extra minutes to ensure the best possible communication.

Communicating via E-Mail

E-mail is no longer an esoteric form of communication that is difficult to use and available only to university faculty and staff. Many large agencies and organizations use e-mail for internal and external communication, and many of us have e-mail via personal computers and connections to the Internet. E-mail makes it easy to dash off quick notes to others. Similar to letters, e-mails typically contain only a small fraction of the information available to us in face-to-face communication. One way people have to overcome this limitation is through the use of what are called *emoticons*, new written ways of conveying emotions. Perhaps the most famous of these is :-), which you see as a smiling face when you tilt your head to the left. Other ways of conveying emotions or emotional reactions on line include using brackets to describe your expression, such as <grin>, or using an acronym such as LOL (short for laughing out loud). What's important when using e-mail is to be as clear as possible. Sarcasm and subtle humor rarely work well in electronic communication and are best avoided. Similar to voice mail, e-mail is unlikely to be confidential and is easy to forward, so it's best to think about the consequences before sending confidential, embarrassing, or negative notes to anyone.

> *The leverage is in the interaction.*
>
> *(Bramson, 1981, p. 143)*

WORKING WITH DIFFICULT PEOPLE

The last part of this chapter concerns the process of interacting with people whose actions you find frustrating. Examples of difficult behavior include the following: the colleague who smiles and nods when you ask her to do something and then does not do it, the supervisor who yells at you when you say that he has not been clear, or your counterpart at another agency who does not return your calls. These are people with whom it is difficult to work. Their behavior may trigger strong emotional reactions in you, reactions that make it hard to behave calmly and proactively. There are three ways you can respond to people who act in problematic ways: 1) You can try to change their behavior, which is likely to be a slow process with no guarantee of success; 2) you can give in; or 3) you can cope. Coping involves contending with people on equal terms and is a way to establish a balance of power in a relationship (Bramson, 1981). People you find difficult to work with may have power over you; coping is a way to establish a balance of power in the relationship so that you can both get on with business (Bramson, 1981).

Suppose you work with someone you find difficult. You are constantly exasperated and frustrated by interactions with this person and, as a result, are unable to complete an important part of your job. You find yourself reacting to this person, rather than planning how to handle difficult situations in advance. Simply reacting will not help you in the long run because it places the difficult person in control. The following steps are designed to help you to proactively cope with the problem.

1. *Is this a consistent problem?* Ask yourself whether the person acts this way all the time or just in the current situation. If the problem is not one you typically have with this person, you may want to sit down with her and ask what is happening. If the problem is a continual one, move on to Step 2.
2. *Get some distance from the situation.* Choose a time and a place that remove you enough so that you can consider the problem calmly. For instance, if your problem is with the person in the office next to yours, then you may want to leave your office and find a quiet place farther away.
3. *Describe in detail, preferably in writing, the behavior of the person you find difficult.* For example, the following is Tyrone's description of a colleague who is a complainer. Every time Tyrone says more than "hello" to him, the colleague has something to complain about. Some of the things the colleague has said recently are as follows:
   • "Have you heard the latest? There's another form to fill out before we can help people."
   • "This coffee is terrible. Someone must be dumping motor oil in it."
   • "That client is just going to take our money and gamble it away, and there isn't a thing we can do about it."
   • "The boss is at it again. Now she wants us to have a goal-planning session. What a waste of time!"
4. *Ask yourself how important it is that this situation change.* We all have to make decisions daily about where to invest our time and energy. Consider whether this particular situation is worth investing your time and energy in trying to change it. If yes, continue.
5. *Describe what you did and how you felt when faced with the behavior you listed.* Describe your own actions in as much detail as possible. Here are some of Tyrone's sample responses to the complaints listed previously:
   • "I don't think the new form is so bad."

- "Yes, the coffee does taste pretty bad."
- "Well, we don't have any rules about how our clients spend the money."
- "The session is a nice break in the routine."

  Tyrone also noted he felt frustrated and angry at having to listen to all those complaints.

6. *Review the interactions and emotional reactions you described*, and answer these questions:
   a. *What did you want to accomplish during those interactions?* Tyrone wants to avoid unpleasantness, to stop further complaints, and to feel less frustrated and angry.
   b. *What did you do that seemed to work?* That is, what did you do to make progress toward accomplishing your goals? Tyrone did avoid further unpleasantness in each individual interaction, but he was not successful at ending the other person's complaining, and he still felt frustrated and angry.
   c. *What did you do that did not seem to work?*
7. Given your answers to Step 6, describe what you need to do to cope more effectively. Answer these questions:
   a. *What skills do I need to use that I already have?* Tyrone is able to stay calm and pleasant in response to the complaints, and he is able to identify the positive aspects of unpleasant situations.
   b. *What skills do I need to learn in order to cope with this problem?* Tyrone clearly needs to learn skills that will stop the complaining permanently. According to Bramson (1981), these skills are as follows: listening attentively to the complaint; checking your perception of how the person feels by paraphrasing; and not agreeing or apologizing, even when the complaint is legitimate. In addition, state the facts and acknowledge them, but do not comment; try to move to a problem-solving mode; and if all else fails, ask how the complainer wants the conversation to end because you have another commitment in a few minutes.

   When people behave in ways that do not make sense to you, they are probably getting something out of their behavior (Scott, 1990) and/or do not know how to behave differently. For instance, some complaints are efforts to avoid new tasks. Developing skills in analyzing what people get from engaging in difficult behavior will help you come up with effective coping strategies.

   Another useful skill for coping with difficult people is the ability to work through your emotional reactions to their behavior (Scott, 1990). For instance, if you find yourself thinking that this person is deliberately trying to get your goat, check whether the behavior occurs in interactions with others. If it does, then remind yourself that you are not being singled out. Also, identifying when your emotional reaction to difficult behavior is related to your personal history is very important to developing better coping skills. Suppose you recognize that you feel anxious when people raise their voices because as a child your parents yelled at you when they were drinking. That gives you the information you need to acknowledge that some of your feelings may be about the past rather than about the present situation. Because dealing with difficult people usually involves strong emotions, stress management skills are also crucial (see Chapter 8).

When coping with difficult people, it is important not to get stuck in thinking that everything would be fixed if only these people would do what they "should" do. It is true that if everyone behaved well, then the world would be a better place. Knowing that, however, does not solve the problem, and you are the only person whose behavior you can change directly, so your coping strategy has to be based on what you can do and say, not what you think other people should do.

8. Using your answers to Step 7, *write an action plan that specifies what you will do and when you will do it.*
9. *Set a time to review your progress toward an effective coping strategy.* When you conduct your review, decide whether your plan is working. If not, revise it.

(From Bramson, R.M. (1981). *Coping with difficult people.* Copyright © 1981 by Robert M. Bramson. Adapted by permission of Doubleday, a division of Bantam Doubleday Dell Publishing Group, Inc.)

COPING STRATEGY IN ACTION

Ethel is a "sniper." Whenever Amanda makes a suggestion at a meeting, Ethel has a comment such as "There goes our college graduate again, being high and mighty and trying to improve us." These comments are always made with a smile and a pleasant tone of voice, so they are not openly hostile. Ethel is also a master at making snide remarks about the boss whenever he is not present. A recent example is "Well, he certainly was pleasant today in the staff meeting—I wonder what extra work he's dreaming up for us." When Amanda presented a new approach to delivering one type of service, Ethel said, "There goes Amanda, playing up to the boss again."

Amanda developed a coping plan for working with Ethel. Here are her responses to the nine questions listed in the previous section:

1. *Is this a consistent problem?* Yes, it is. Ethel snipes all the time.
2. *Get some distance from the situation.* Amanda finds an empty conference room and puts a "Meeting in Progress—Do Not Disturb" sign on the door.
3. *Describe the behavior.* Amanda generates the descriptions of Ethel's behavior given above.
4. *How important is it that this situation change?* Very. I have to deal with Ethel every day.
5. *Describe your reactions.* When Ethel said, "There goes our college graduate again," I turned red, muttered something about "just trying to contribute to the team," and shut up. When Ethel made the crack about playing up to the boss, I became angry but did not say anything and soon after left for the women's restroom to regain control of my temper.
6. *What did you want to accomplish?* I wanted to control my temper and shut her up. I did manage to control my temper, except for turning red, but she never shuts up. Failure to respond emotionally seems to help me gain control, but it doesn't prevent future attacks.
7. *Describe what you need to do.* Clearly I need to continue to control my emotions while learning a way to prevent ongoing attacks. I think I need to be more direct with Ethel. I also need to consider what she might be getting out of her behavior. She gets to see my emotional reaction—I wonder if she says those nasty things to get attention.
8. *Write an action plan.* Here is my plan. The next time she snipes at me in a staff meeting, I'm going to address her directly by saying something like, "Ethel, that sounds like you're making fun of me. Is that what you mean to do?" She will probably deny that she is making fun, but that's okay. The other thing she might do is tell me that what I'm suggesting is all wrong and why. If she does that, I'll try to find out what everyone else thinks, for example by asking, "Does anyone else agree with that point of view?" If others agree there is a problem with my idea, then I'll suggest we try to solve it. It's okay for her to criticize my ideas as long as the criticism is open and can be discussed. It's not okay for her to snipe at me. I suppose one other way she could react is to agree that she is making fun of me. If she does, I'll tell her that, like most people, I don't like being made fun of, and I'll ask whether she's willing to stop. If she admits publicly to making fun of me, then I think it's okay to put her on the spot.

My biggest problem with this plan will be staying calm, because I see red when Ethel snipes. I'll try to take a slow, deep breath before I make any response to her sniping.

I guess my plan won't work if she snipes because it's the only way she has to get attention. She does have good ideas sometimes. Maybe I'll also try to approach her and ask her advice at times when she's not sniping. It's not that I want to avoid her altogether; I just don't want to be treated badly.

9. *Set a time to review your progress toward an effective coping strategy.* I'll review the situation in 3 weeks and decide whether I've made any progress.

This coping strategy often helps, but it does not lead to success every time you use it. Sometimes your best efforts to cope fail. Then, it is time to remember that you always have a choice about whether you continue to stay in contact with a person whose behavior is consistently difficult (Bramson, 1981). This is not an easy choice, particularly when your difficult person is your supervisor and your only choice is to find another job. Choosing to withdraw from contact, however, is always your final option.

> *Cherish an awareness that coping with Difficult People is never easy and hardly ever fun. If you know what you're doing, you ought to feel uneasy. Acknowledgment of fear is the first step toward moving beyond it.*
>
> *(Bramson, 1981, p. 175)*

Exercise

6-7. Pick one difficult person you must interact with regularly at work or at school. Use the nine steps above to develop a plan for coping with that person.

FURTHER TALES OF DIANA

The group is meeting for the first time since everyone has done the exercises in Chapter 6. Diana says, "Sometimes I wonder how we manage to communicate at all. I spent part of this morning with an adolescent who misunderstood everything I said and then went to a staff meeting where people seemed determined not to listen to each other. I wanted to make them all start paraphrasing immediately!

"Akram," she goes on, "what part of the chapter hit home for you?"

"Oh, that's easy," he replies, "I want to require everyone who calls me to take a class in leaving voice mail messages that make sense. It sure would make my life easier. How about you, Hunter?"

Hunter grimaces. "I'm working on a plan for coping with a difficult co-worker. The strategy makes sense, and I've got to get better at dealing with this person, but doing it is not going to be fun. All expressions of sympathy will be gratefully appreciated."

Everyone makes soothing noises, and the meeting adjourns.

CHAPTER 7

Professional Development
or
Find Your Job, and Love It

OBJECTIVES

- Describe the characteristics of the ideal job for you.

- Prepare the materials needed to apply for a position.

- Prepare for a professional interview.

- Begin creating formal and informal professional development opportunities.

*It is possible to work 10 years and have either 10 years of
experience or 1 year of experience 10 times.*

(Anonymous)

The person who gets 10 years of experience in 10 years has never
stopped learning. The person who has had 1 year of experience 10
times learned to do things in a certain way the first year on the job and
continued to do them the same way for the next 9 years. This chapter
is about becoming the professional who never stops learning and improving her professional skills.

There are many ways to develop professionally. One is to find a
job in your field that will give you the opportunity to learn and grow.
Another way to develop professionally is to enter a degree program
in a community college, an undergraduate college or university, or a
graduate school. Also, you may choose to develop your knowledge
and skills through experiences that do not involve degree programs.
These may include specialized training programs, certificate programs,
seminars, or nondegree or noncredit college courses as well as self-
created educational or personal growth experiences. Most people
choose some combination of degree programs, on-the-job training,
and/or specialized training during their careers. The focus of this
chapter is on 1) helping you find a job in which you are able to grow
and 2) non–degree-based professional development.

Heidi Daly

I would suggest to people that are thinking of going into
human services to look into the different fields before you even
do an internship, because the internship that you choose definitely steers you toward where you are going. You get that experience and then the jobs that you are looking for will look at
that experience and want to use that experience you've had. So
it's very important to try to figure out exactly what you want to
do, at least what you think you want to do. Go talk to people in
the different types of fields, whatever you want to go into. [Ask
them] what kind of barriers did they come across, what are the
positives, and what are the negatives. I would highly recommend that before you start anything.

William Esp

When I went to school I had no idea that they had this
addictions program there. Being a recovering person, I never
had any intent to ever be an addictions counselor, nor would I

have ever predicted that's what I would have ended up doing. I was just going to get certification. I never even thought I'd get a bachelor's degree. Once I got in school I fell in love with it, I fell in love with the human services department. Compared to the other departments it was really experiential—they had practicums and internships, which a lot of undergraduate programs don't have. Up until that point my recovery was pretty much focused within 12-step programs, and school just really opened me up to a lot of new thinking about recovery, about addictions. So in a sense I fell into it.

I'm finishing my master's as we speak—I just handed in my thesis and am wrapping up my internship. It's in counseling psychology, in transpersonal psychology. Because of my addictions background, I just have a really strong belief in the spiritual aspect of healing and recovery. They have a Jungian component to the program, and I love Jungian psychology. I eventually will get my LPC (Licensed Professional Counselor), and I would like to do private work while probably staying affiliated with the hospital. (That remains to be seen because right now it's undergoing such a weird transition with managed care.)

FINDING A JOB

Before you begin looking for work, ask yourself a few basic questions:

1. *What type of work do you want to do?* Be specific about the types of activities in which you are interested, the characteristics of the consumers you wish to serve, and what you want to accomplish.
2. *Under what conditions are you willing to work?* Where are you willing to live? Are you willing to be a live-in staff member? Are you willing to relocate? What hours are you willing to work?
3. *What salary and benefits do you expect to receive?* How much will you settle for? Which benefits are most important?

Your Résumé

There are many approaches to putting together a professional résumé. The design you choose is probably less important than the information you include. Following is a list of information that you should include on your résumé.

Employment History   Include exact dates of all relevant positions, job titles, employer names, and brief descriptions of your responsibilities in the employment history section. Do not give only the year you held a previous job, because the employer cannot tell whether you held the job for 1 day or the entire year. Instead, use a phrase such as "From 1/97 to 2/99."

Educational History   Include dates of all degrees, dates of attendance in relevant programs from which you did not receive a degree, and the names of all educational institutions attended in the educational history section. Also include any other specialized or technical training (e.g., psychiatric technician) that may be of interest to an employer. For instance, list a 2-month undergraduate internship at a community mental health center if you are applying for a position in a treatment program for people with chronic mental illnesses.

Other Relevant Information   Please note the emphasis on the word "relevant." Volunteer work is relevant if you acquired or refined a job-related skill. Volunteer experience can also tell the employer about characteristics such as commitment and reliability. Some employers find information about special interests, activities, and awards helpful in giving them a feel for the person.

Information to Omit from Your Résumé   Do not include the following details on your résumé: your age, gender, height, weight, religion, marital status, ethnicity, state of health, ages and names of children, hobbies, or any other personal information. If personal information is relevant to the job, then the employer should tell you it is relevant when asking for it. If it is not relevant to the job, then it is probably illegal for the employer to ask you for it. Furthermore, it is worth remembering that an employer who will hire you on the basis of your personal characteristics might also fire you on the same basis.

Finally, the author recommends against heading your résumé with a career objective or goal (some career counselors disagree). Most of the objectives found on résumés are either so broad as to be meaningless or so specific that they do not apply to most positions. Broad career goals do not, in the author's opinion, improve the likelihood that the employer will want to interview you. Of course you want to "serve people and to maximize your professional growth," so why bother to state the obvious?

Occasionally, a career objective is stated specifically. The problem with concrete objectives is that job applicants tend to misuse them. If you have a concrete objective on your résumé, you should use that version of your résumé to apply *only* for positions that will help you to achieve that objective; similarly, you should have different versions of your résumé available for different types of positions. If you apply for a job that does not fit with your career objective, the employer is justified in wondering how serious you are about the position.

One possible résumé format is shown in Figure 1.

Rebecca J. Allen

Office: 727 E. Third
         Anywhere, ZZ 11111
         (000) XXX-XXXX

Home: 1433 North Boulevard
        Anywhere, ZZ 11112
        (000) XXX-XXXX

PROFESSIONAL EXPERIENCE

Family Services Agency
727 E. Third, Anywhere, ZZ 11111

7/96–present   Position: Program Supervisor
                  Responsibilities: Include all those listed below as well as supervising six program managers and representing the agency at intake meetings

9/94–6/96   Position: Program Manager
                  Responsibilities: Maintain a caseload of 14 children in 10 foster homes; provide bimonthly home visits to monitor child needs and progress; train foster parents in treatment implementation; maintain regular documentation; arrange for necessary medical services; coordinate services with schools, social services, and social security; provide crisis resolution as needed

Child Treatment Services
1500 South Hill Street, Somewhere, BB 99999

6/93–8/94   Position: Treatment Staff
                  Responsibilities: Implementation of treatment plans for six children ages 7–10 in residential treatment facility; work closely with other team members, including agency social worker, families of children in treatment, and consulting psychologist

EDUCATIONAL EXPERIENCE

9/93–5/94   University of My State
               Bachelor of Social Work, magna cum laude, May 1994
9/90–8/93   City State College

CONTINUING EDUCATION

Attended training seminars on goal planning in child services, legal issues, and professional communication

PROFESSIONAL ORGANIZATIONS

My State Association of Child Social Workers
7/97–present   full member
                              membership chairperson

PROFESSIONAL REFERENCES

John Chee, Executive Director
Family Services Agency
Anywhere, ZZ
(000) XXX-XXXX

Samuel Marshall, Ph.D.
Department of Social Work
University of My State
Anywhere, ZZ
(000) XXX-XXXX

Margaret Barolo, Treatment Supervisor
Child Treatment Services
Somewhere, BB
(000) XXX-XXXX

Figure 1. Résumé: Rebecca J. Allen.

Exercise

7-1.   If you do not have a résumé, write one. If you do have a résumé, then review it, and make any needed revisions to bring it up to date.

Letters of Application

The importance of the letter of application cannot be overstated. The letter of application, along with your résumé, is your first contact with a possible employer. There are a variety of guides to writing good letters: Use one if you are not sure of your ability to put together a good letter. Your public library is a good place to find helpful guides, as is the career development section of your local bookstore. If you want to make a good first impression, then be sure you do the following:

1.   Make an effort to obtain the full name of the agency director or personnel director to whom your letter will be addressed.
2.   Type your letters! It is amazing how many people apply for professional positions with handwritten notes. If you do not have a typewriter, a word processor, or a computer, borrow or rent one or pay to have your letters typed. Public libraries and some photocopying shops often have typewriters or computers available for patrons.
3.   Proofread your résumé. If you are not a good speller, then have someone who is proofread it. If you use a software program to check your spelling, remember it will not find words that shouldn't be there but are spelled correctly.
4.   If you find an error, then fix it, and print a corrected copy.
5.   Use a copy machine or printer that will give you clean copies of your résumé, copies that are as clear as the original.
6.   Avoid sending obvious copies (rather than originals) of your letter of application. If you are using a computer, use letter-quality print, preferably on a laser or ink-jet printer and be sure each letter is personally addressed to its recipient. It is a major faux pas to type a letter and write the recipient's name in by hand. You may not be taken seriously if it is obvious that you have sent out a bulk mailing of letters and résumés.

Exercise

7-2.   Imagine finding an ad for the position of your dreams. Write a letter of application designed to convince the addressee that you are the best person for the position. You may use only the qualifications and experience you actually have. A sample is shown in Figure 2.

Your References

Your résumé should list names, addresses, and telephone numbers for at least three references, or it should indicate that references are available upon request. If you do not list references on your résumé, then have a typed list of them ready to give to a prospective employer when you go for an interview. Your first choice for references should be supervisors or other authorities who have been in a position to observe your skills and abilities. Former professors or colleagues may also be appropriate. Individuals who can attest to your character but not to your professional skills cannot hurt, but they may not help much. Get permission from all those whom you want to use as references before giving out their names.

You may choose not to list your current or immediate past supervisor because you expect that person to give you a negative reference.

1234 Main Street
Anytown, CC 99999
November 17, 1998

Helge Sampson, Executive Director
Main Street Placement Agency
555 Central Avenue
Anytown, CC 99999

Dear Ms. Sampson:

I am writing to apply for the Job Placement Specialist position you advertised in the *Metro Times* yesterday.

I believe you will find me well-qualified for the position. I have recently completed my Bachelor of Science in Vocational Rehabilitation and have 3 years of direct experience working as a job placement specialist. I'm interested in working for Main Street Placement Agency because the agency is well-known for its high-quality services.

Enclosed is a copy of my résumé. I look forward to hearing from you at your earliest convenience. I can be reached at work during weekdays, (000) XXX-XXXX, and at home at other times, (000) XXX-XXXX.

Sincerely,

Martin J. Duran

Figure 2.   Letter of application: Martin J. Duran.

If so, be prepared to respond to an interviewer who asks why you omitted that person's name from the list. It is best to be honest without going into great detail if you are asked this question. For instance, you might say, "I felt Ms. Lee would not describe my skills as favorably as the people I did list because we had several disagreements about appropriate treatment for my clients." Do *not* say any more! If you are asked for additional details, politely suggest that you would prefer not to dwell on the issue. Going on at great length about how you were mistreated in a previous position is a grave mistake, both because it creates a negative impression and because the interviewer might have a personal connection with your former supervisor.

The Interview

Preparing for the Interview   You will create an excellent first impression in an interview if you do some homework about the agency before you go. Find out about it by asking for materials such as brochures, asking other agencies, asking friends in human services, and looking for information about the agency on the World Wide Web. If you walk into the interview with some knowledge of the agency's goals and programs, you have demonstrated your interest in the position to the interviewer.

Imagine how you might answer the questions an interviewer is likely to ask. For instance, how will you describe your strengths? How will you describe your weaknesses? Are any of your strengths also weaknesses? Are weaknesses also strengths? For example, maybe you tend to focus on just one project at a time, which means that you sometimes let other work pile up, but it may also mean that you are good at finishing what you start.

The employer's first impression of you is based on your letter of application and your résumé. The first impression you create at the interview is equally important. Your task is to convince the employer that you are serious about the position. There are two easy ways to do this. One is to *arrive on time*. Few mistakes are as deadly as arriving late for an interview. No one will ever fault you for being 15 minutes early, so plan plenty of time to cope with unexpected traffic delays or late buses. Also, if you are a few minutes early, you will have time to catch your breath and become more comfortable before the interview begins. The second easy way to create a good impression is to *dress up for the interview*. Makeup and cologne, if used, should be subdued. In general, you should plan to dress more formally for the interview than you would for the job.

During the Interview   Take the time to answer questions thoughtfully and carefully. Make eye contact with the interviewer regularly, and offer a firm handshake when you introduce yourself and another at the end of the interview. Listen carefully to the interviewer's name and title and ask for them again if needed. Then, call the interviewer by her or his last name unless invited to do otherwise (i.e., Ms., Mr., or Dr. Whatever). It is always better to be too formal than to be too informal. If you are being interviewed by two or more people, then be equally polite and formal with all of them. Never make assumptions about who will make the hiring decision. One common mistake is being respectful and formal when interacting with a male interviewer but informal and familiar with a female team member who happens to be the boss!

Perhaps the two most important things you have to tell an employer in an interview are 1) why you want that particular job and 2) which of your skills and abilities will be beneficial to the agency. The interviewer is interested in what you have to offer the organization, so you need to tell that person what you have to offer before there is any mention of what the organization has to offer you. Your first response to "Why are you interested in this position?" should *not* be "I am starting back to school and the hours fit well with my class schedule," "I need a change," or "The salary is attractive." Those statements may well be true, but most employers will not be pleased if your convenience is your primary motive for wanting the job. A better answer would be something such as "Your program has a reputation for providing good services for people and good working conditions for staff. I think I can make a contribution here and learn from you."

You should be prepared to answer questions about why you want to leave your current position and what you see as your professional strengths and weaknesses. You may also be given descriptions of specific client needs and asked how you will meet those needs. Many employers in human services will ask you whether you are willing to make a commitment to the position of at least a year. You may also be asked whether you are willing to work evenings or weekends or whether you will work in a setting that bans smoking (it is usually legal to ban smoking, and in some states a ban is required by law in government offices).

In many places it is not legal for an employer to ask you questions about your political or religious convictions. Furthermore, it is often illegal to ask a woman whether she is pregnant, to ask her whether she intends to become pregnant in the near future, or to ask anyone anything related to child care.

On Interviewing the Interviewer   There are two main purposes for an employment interview. One is for the employer to find out whether you are right not only for the job but also for the organization. The other is for you to find out whether the employer is right for you.

The best way to do this is to make a list of characteristics important to you as well as questions about the agency that come up when you respond to the interviewer (see the previous discussion about preparing). Take the list with you to the interview, and toward the end ask for any information you want that you have not already been given. This is the time to ask about salaries, but do not try to negotiate until and unless you have been offered the job. Also, you can learn quite a bit about an agency by careful observation. Observe the physical surroundings and how members of the professional staff interact with those they serve, with each other, and with support staff.

After the Interview   If, after the interview, you are still seriously interested in the position, then follow up with a brief note restating your interest in the position and thanking the interviewer for taking the time to consider you. Even if you are not interested in the position, you may wish to send a thank-you letter to establish a positive relationship with the interviewer and/or the agency. Again, the letter should be typed. Because you will have met the person to whom the letter is addressed, it is crucial to have that person's correct name and title on the letter. If necessary, call to confirm the name, title, and spelling. Follow-up letters should be positive but not effusive (words such as *thrilled* and *ecstatic* are effusive). A sample letter is shown in Figure 3.

Follow-up telephone calls are usually not a good idea, because you may be seen as overly eager. The exception to this rule is in the

---

                                              1234 Main Street
                                              Anytown, CC 99999
                                              November 25, 1998

Helge Sampson, Executive Director
Main Street Placement Agency
555 Central Avenue
Anytown, CC 99999

Dear Ms. Sampson:

    I want to thank you again for the opportunity to meet with you and the placement staff this morning. I do feel I could make a positive contribution to your program and look forward to hearing from you in the near future.

Sincerely,

Martin J. Duran

Figure 3.   Thank-you letter: Martin J. Duran

case where you have been told you will be contacted by a certain date and no contact has been made. In that case, it is reasonable to call and ask whether a decision has been made.

Exercise

7-3. Make a list of the following:
   a. Important things you want to ask when you interview for a job
   b. Important characteristics you want to look for in an organization when you go for an interview (e.g., amount of supervision and feedback that is provided, opportunity for advancement, opportunities for professional development)

PLANNING FOR PROFESSIONAL DEVELOPMENT

An unanswered question is a fine traveling companion. It sharpens your eye for the road.

(Remen, 1996, p. 293)

Before you can plan for your professional development, you must be able to distinguish what you can do and do know from what you cannot do and do not know. You may need or want to learn skills required for your present responsibilities as well as skills that allow you to expand professionally. Identifying skills you need to perform your current job can be unpleasant because it involves admitting that you may have made mistakes or that there are things you do not know. Many professionals find it difficult to objectively review their own skills and identify their own deficiencies. This is unfortunate, for none of us know everything we need or want to know.

In the course of planning for your professional development, it is important to remember the difference between knowledge and skills. If you want to find out about new approaches to counseling or the latest research on serving people with physical disabilities, then you are interested in acquiring new knowledge. If you want to learn how to use a new therapeutic technique, then you are interested in learning new skills. Classes and lectures are good ways to increase your knowledge. The only effective way to learn a new skill is to find someone who has the skill and will provide you with lots of feedback about technique, what you are doing correctly, and what you need to change. The person who gives you feedback and suggests new directions for growth is often called a *mentor*. Observing someone effectively using the skill you want to learn is helpful, but this is not a substitute for getting feedback on your own performance.

It can be difficult, particularly in small agencies or in small communities, to find opportunities for professional development. Funds are rarely available to send you to formal training programs, especially when these are not available locally. Fortunately there are a variety of alternative ways to grow and learn. The following sections list commonly used formal and informal ways to develop professionally.

Professional development sometimes takes us in unexpected directions. Just because you started out with training in one profession or one type of work, you don't have to stay in it for the rest of your life. Life span keeps increasing, and it is common to have more than one career in a lifetime, often three or more. Don't be afraid to explore possible career changes or new directions that interest you. You'll do a better job if you develop in directions that interest you than if you do what others tell you is sensible.

Formal Approaches to Professional Development

Join a Professional Organization Professional organizations offer several paths to development. Many of them publish journals or newsletters that can keep you abreast of current developments in your field. Most professional organizations hold annual conventions where you may hear speakers and meet other people who share your interests. The larger organizations usually have state and/or regional chapters that hold annual meetings closer to home and are therefore less expensive to attend than national meetings. Many organizations provide information and contact with other professionals via home pages on the World Wide Web. Some professional groups also offer continuing education programs and send notices to all members. Another benefit of membership in a large national professional group is that other organizations and publishers often buy their mailing lists. Thus, if you belong to one group, then you are likely to get notices of meetings and new materials from many different sources.

There are hundreds of professional human services organizations in the United States and many more around the world. A selection of these are listed in the appendix at the end of this chapter.

Go Back to School There are a great variety of college and university programs aimed at the working professional. In many locations there are programs that offer classes primarily in evenings and on weekends so that people who work full time are able to attend. There are also programs that allow you to attend full time for a few weeks every year and do the remainder of your work via mail or the Internet. If you are interested in going back to school part time, then speak with other people in your field, and consult the resources of your professional organizations and your public library to determine what is available. Also, find out whether your employer offers any financial support or other incentives for additional schooling.

Suzanne Cardiff

Ten years ago I never would have said I'd be doing this job, so I don't like to plan too far ahead. I kind of go with the flow, what's offered to me. I try to take as many trainings as offered. I like to learn as much as I can. I do want to go back to school; I don't want to stay in social services.

Since I was yea high, I've wanted to be a teacher. Now I'm just getting life experiences before I go to school for my teaching degree. This way I'm going to have a bigger edge than most people who go into teaching before they get to see stuff like this.

Attend Workshops and Seminars   If you live in a metropolitan area, chances are you will find numerous opportunities to attend short workshops and seminars. These programs usually range from a few hours to several days in length and can cost anywhere from $50 or $60 to $500 or more for a 4- or 5-day course. The quality of short workshops and seminars can vary widely. Before you invest your time and money, particularly if you will have to travel and pay for lodging, try to find other professionals who have attended courses given by the same instructors. Ask them what topics were covered and what they got out of those courses (they may not have wanted to learn what you want to, so it is important to ask what was done as well as whether it met their needs). Many human services agencies do have budgets (not large) for staff development and may be willing to pay part or all of the cost of a workshop or course. Both formal college and university courses as well as seminars and workshops are now available via a variety of distance learning technologies, so even if you are in a rural location you will still have access to numerous opportunities for professional development.

Jennifer Echarte

I'm going to massage school now to get trained as a massage therapist because touch is something that is important to me.

I have gotten a very good idea of the systems here and I've thought about getting my LCSW. I'm going to move on to family preservation services and see what that's like. I'm going to learn more about the human body through this massage work that I'm doing, so [I] get the anatomy/physiology part. I'm going to take a neuroscience class to get the chemistry of the brain. So I've got nature and nurture, and from that I really am not certain which route I want to take. I've been thinking more of going toward education with this same population.

Pamela Meister

I feel like I'm in the very initial stages of what this job will mean to me personally. One of the areas of focus, and I think it is going to be nationally as well, is educating physicians about their need to have some customer service skills. That's really exciting for me because that's one of our higher areas of complaint. It's not so much the doctor did anything that was even close to malpractice, but it would be things such as "I went in and saw the doctor, and the doctor didn't even make eye contact with me," or "I don't feel like they really cared, they were really in a hurry," or "I had other things to tell them and they didn't even ask. How can they make a diagnosis when maybe they don't have all the facts?" What we're trying to educate doctors to see is that if they connect with that person, they can have an error. If there is an error and they have that rapport, the patient's probably going to say, "I know you really tried, and I know this happened, but hey you're such a nice doctor, that's okay. I'll let you go on this one." We're trying to get that across.

Johnn Young

Originally I did medical care and then I also decided I wanted to do something to help the community, so I decided to go and help at the gay, lesbian, and bisexual services center. Then after being in the health care field for about 15 years, I decided I need to do something else. I was taking all these courses and getting all these certifications and decided one day when they mispronounced my name at a long-time employee dinner, it was time to do something else. They pronounced it JoAnn instead of Johnn, and I go, I think after 15 years, I need to quit. That was it, that was the day I quit.

I've decided that I will probably stay with what I'm doing for the rest of my life. Whether or not I'll be doing it with HIV prevention, I don't know, it just depends on the course of the epidemic. I want to go back to school. I spend a lot of my personal time trying to figure out what do I want to do when I grow up, and the answer to that is always be happy. What do I need to get there, this whole planning for professional development question, that's a hard question for me. I guess whatever my heart calls me to do will be the direction I'm taking because then it's never wrong.

Informal Approaches to Professional Development

Use Your Library   Almost every public and university library in the country has the ability to help you request a computer search on a topic of interest to you. Usually the library has a staff member who can advise you of the cost and can help you list descriptor words for your topic and decide which databases to search. These searches result in a list of references on the topic of interest. Then, if your local library does not have the references you want, it probably has an interlibrary loan department that will search nationally for your reference. College or university libraries have current journals rooms where you can browse through a variety of publications at no cost. Most libraries also offer Internet access (sometime free, but not always) so that you can conduct your own on-line searches. You can also use the Internet to look for World Wide Web pages in areas of interest, join mailing lists about professional issues, and chat with human services professionals from all over the world.

Learn from Your Colleagues   Almost everyone with whom you work has a skill that may be useful to you. Observe your colleagues, and ask yourself what results they achieve and which skills they have that you value. Then, ask them for help in learning those skills. This can be a touchy request because it means asking people to look at your deficits rather than your strengths. The constructive criticism that is easiest to hear and use, as discussed in Chapter 6, is proactive feedback. That is, ask your colleagues to tell you what skills you need to use more often, not what is awful and what you should stop doing.

Ellen Berlin

There was a book when I was at home [raising children] called *Sequencing*, I think, that reinforced [for] me that you can go through your life and do it in bits and pieces. I know some people stay home when their little people are littler, and I have a friend who is staying home now when her children are bigger.

I'm challenged by reaching out. I just am a firm believer in always learning, always reading. To find time to take a class, because of how I juggle all these other little work experiences, that's been a hard one for me. And then also deciding to put money into that has been interesting at this point in my life, but as far as stimulating my own growth so I can feel that I'm on top of things and also stay excited happens a lot through reading for me. I'm always reading. It's been wonderful—I'm always doing lots of growing with that.

Find a Mentor   A mentor is a trusted counselor, guide, tutor, or coach, someone who can help you develop professionally. This person is therefore usually someone who has more skill, knowledge, or expertise than you do in at least one area of professional functioning. A mentor can teach you implicitly or explicitly. Implicit teaching is teaching by example: You watch the person and observe what he does. Explicit teaching is just that: The mentor instructs you and gives you feedback on how well you are doing.

You cannot require anyone to be your mentor, particularly when you would like them to teach you explicitly. You can, however, carefully observe people you meet during work, both within and outside of your agency (don't forget your supervisor is a potential mentor), and look for those people with skills or characteristics you wish to acquire. You may identify a prospective mentor by approaching an individual who has a specific skill you want to learn, or that person may possess something more global, such as a style you want to emulate. You are most likely to learn from a person you see as similar to you in some way.

Once you have found a possible mentor, ask for assistance. Most professionals, if they can spare the time, are happy to help less experienced colleagues broaden their skills. Mentors can help you to expand your perspective on services delivery and examine future options that are different from your present position. One caution about mentors: Nearly all of us need more than one mentor during the course of our careers, and we often need more than one mentor at the same time. No one person is likely to have all the answers or to provide a complete overview of all the possibilities open to you.

Start a Network   Perhaps you work in a very small agency with only a handful of other staff members. You may want to learn skills that none of your co-workers will be able to teach you. In that case, start finding ways to learn from your colleagues at other agencies. There are a variety of ways to proceed, from having lunch periodically with one or more people from other organizations, to actually starting a local or state chapter of a professional organization, to joining or starting an electronic discussion group.

As you look for ways to add to your skills, keep in mind that practical experience and learning of abstract principles are both important in acquiring skills. In addition, assessment that tells you whether you really do understand new material is important ("Academy Releases Report," 1994).

Exercises

7-4. By talking to other people in your field, going to the library, searching the Internet, or writing for information, find out about at least two professional organizations or university programs that might contribute to your professional development.

7-5. Do at least one of the following:
   a. Arrange for a computer search on a topic of professional interest.
   b. Identify a skill one of your colleagues (e.g., a co-worker, a supervisor, a support staff member, a person from another department) could teach you that you want to learn. Arrange to learn that skill from the person you have chosen.
   c. Identify at least two people who work in other agencies in your community who have skills you want to learn. Meet with them to discuss your interest.

Christa Pavlus

Well, I've gone back and forth. I was a staff therapist, and I was a supervising therapist in the building. Then I went on to be a director, and when I finished having the baby, that wasn't working. So, I came back to being a staff therapist. I am a supervising therapist and maybe someday would like to go back to a director position, but I think that I would like to get into more directing program development.

Cathy Phelps

I always am open to opportunities to do other things. Being able to teach has been a good thing, leading a long-term support group, doing some consulting for a group, a social work team, that was really exciting. It was fun for me to learn African dance and American Sign Language. Working on a book on sexual assault and HIV, that fell into my lap. I was interested in that because it's talking about women's risk for that kind of thing. So then learning more about that and also testing my writing skills was good.

I teach at the community college, and they have a victim assistance certification program. Some of [the students] already have bachelor-level degrees, but they're just going into victim assistance. A lot of them are students who are adults returning to school, and they're in law enforcement, some of them are teachers, some of them are early childhood education majors, some people are interested in psychology, sociology.

A FINAL NOTE ON PROFESSIONAL DEVELOPMENT

It is natural to want to focus on the parts of your job that are rewarding, including those activities that result in your professional growth. Do remember, as you plan for your professional development, that your employer's priorities for you may be different from your own. Most employers support professional development, but they expect employees to fulfill basic responsibilities first.

MORE TALES OF DIANA

By their next meeting everyone in Diana's group has read the first seven chapters of *"Human services? . . . That must be so rewarding"* and has worked through the exercises in those chapters. Diana, smiling, tells the group, "I was so close to leaving human services before we started meeting. This book has helped me really look at who I am and why I am a probation officer.

"Best of all, having the support of this group has helped me take charge of my professional career. It's so reassuring to know that other people have the same problems and get the same rewards I do. I'm going to work through the next chapter on stress management, but I feel like this group is one of my best ways to take care of myself! Would you be willing to keep meeting once a month to keep that support going?"

The group agrees to continue meeting, and Hunter offers to host the next session, saying, "It's great being part of this motley crew—I've actually tried some of this stuff, and it helps my attitude toward my job a whole lot."

Professional Organizations

American Association for
   Marriage and Family
   Therapy
1133 15th Street, NW, Suite 300
Washington, D.C. 20005
202-452-0109; FAX: 202-223-2329
http://www.aamft.org/

American Association of
   Pastoral Counselors
9504A Lee Highway
Fairfax, VA 22031
703-385-6967; FAX: 703-352-7725
http://www.metanoia.org/
   aapc/

American Association of
   Psychiatric Technicians
2059 South Third Street
Niles, MI 49120
800-391-7589
http://www.aapt.com/

American Association on
   Mental Retardation
444 North Capitol Street, NW,
   Suite 846
Washington, D.C. 20001
800-424-3688; 202-387-1968;
   FAX: 202-387-2193
http://www.aamr.org/

American Federation of
   Teachers
555 New Jersey Avenue, NW
Washington, D.C. 20001
202-879-4400
http://www.aft.org/

American Mental Health
   Counselors Association
801 North Fairfax Street,
   Suite 304
Alexandria, VA 22314
703-548-6002; FAX: 202-387-2193
http://www.pie.org/amhca

American Occupational
   Therapy Association
4720 Montgomery Lane
Bethesda, MD 20814
301-652-2682; FAX: 301-652-
   7711
http://www.aota.org/

American Physical Therapy
   Association
1111 North Fairfax Street
Alexandria, VA 22314
703-684-APTA [703-684-2782];
   FAX: 703-684-7343
http://www.apta.org/

American Psychiatric Nurses
   Association
1200 19th Street, NW, Suite 300
Washington, D.C. 20036
202-857-1133; FAX: 202-223-4579
http://www.apna.org/

American Psychological
   Association
750 First Street, NE
Washington, D.C. 20002
202-336-5500
http://www.apa.org/

American Speech-Language-
   Hearing Association
10801 Rockville Pike
Rockville, MD 20852
800-498-2071; 301-897-5700;
   TTY: 301-897-0157;
   FAX: 301-571-0457
http://www.asha.org

Association for Behavior
   Analysis
Western Michigan University
213 West Hall
1201 Oliver Street
Kalamazoo, MI 49008
616-387-8341; 616-387-8342;
   FAX: 616-387-8354
http://www.wmich.edu/aba/
   index.html

Association for Advancement
   of Behavior Therapy
305 Seventh Avenue
New York, NY 10001
212-647-1890; FAX: 202-647-1865
http://www.aabt.org/aabt/

Council for Exceptional
   Children
1920 Association Drive
Reston, VA 22091
888-CEC-SPED [888-232-7733]
http://www.cec.sped.org/

Employee Assistance Program
   Association
2101 Wilson Boulevard,
   Suite 500
Arlington, VA 22201
703-522-6272; FAX: 703-522-4585
http://www.eap-association.
   com/

Gerontological Society of
   America
1275 K Street, NW, Suite 350
Washington, D.C. 20005
202-842-1275; FAX: 202-842-1150
http://www.geron.org/

National Alliance for Direct
  Support Professionals
c/o Susan O'Neill
Post Office Box 13315
Minneapolis, MN 55414
http://www.ici.coled.umn.ed/
  DSP/

National Association of
  Protection and Advocacy
  Systems
900 Second Street, NE, Suite 211
Washington, D.C. 20002
202-408-9514; TDD: 202-408-
  9521; FAX: 202-408-9520
http://www.protectionandad
  vocacy.com/napas.htm

National Association of Social
  Workers
750 First Street, NE, Suite 700
Washington, D.C. 20005
202-408-8600; FAX: 202-336-8311
http://www.naswdc.org/

National Board for Certified
  Counselors
3 Terrace Way, Suite D
Greensboro, NC 27403
336-547-0607; FAX: 336-547-0017
http://www.nbcc.org/

National Education
  Association
1201 16th Street, NW
Washington, D.C. 20036
202-833-4000

National Rehabilitation
  Association
633 South Washington Street
Alexandria, VA 22314
703-836-0850
http://www.nationalrehab.org/

The American Correctional
  Association
4380 Forbes Boulevard
Lanham, MD 20706
800-222-5646
http://www.corrections.com/
  aca/index.html

The Association for Persons
  with Severe Handicaps
29 West Susquehanna Avenue,
  Suite 210
Baltimore, MD 21204
410-828-8274; FAX: 410-828-6706
http://www.tash.org/

SECTION IV

Again, Human

CHAPTER 8

Stress Management
or

No One Ever Told Me There'd Be Days Like This

If you are alive, then there is stress in your life because stress is your response to any demand put on you (Simmons, 1997). When people talk about being under a great deal of stress, talk about being "stressed out," or say they are "stressing," they mean they are feeling the negative effects of demands placed on them. In human services, professionals who are responding very negatively to stressors often say that they are "burned out." Stress, however, does not have to be consistently negative, nor does it have to have negative effects on you. This chapter is about negative reactions to stressors, what causes the reactions, and how to care for yourself in ways that reduce the impact of negative stress.

The author's basic assumption is that people who work in the human services are "only human." This sounds too obvious to need saying. Consider, however, some common myths about human services workers.

- They are professionals who are above reproach.
- Their work provides them with inherent, infinite personal rewards.
- They are miracle workers.
- They remain calm at all times.
- They subjugate their feelings to those of the people they serve.
- They love all those they serve.
- They have no favorites among those they serve.
- They know all of the answers.
- They cope with life without stress, anxiety, or conflict.

(adapted from Greenberg, 1984)

These myths present us as perfect. They are wrong, silly, and can sometimes be dangerous. Myths become dangerous when we try to live up to them, refusing to acknowledge that we cannot be perfect. In fact, people with jobs that require them to have substantial responsibility for the welfare of others experience an increased incidence of stress-related illnesses (Anderson, 1978). This chapter is about working in human services and being human (but not superhuman).

EFFECTS OF STRESS

We have the same physiological responses to potential dangers that our ancestors had. As in prehistoric cultures, we experience increases in blood sugar and oxygen flow, in blood pressure, and in stomach acid. In extreme cases, adrenaline is released into our bloodstream (McKay, Davis, & Eshelman, 1995). These responses were very adaptive during an earlier evolutionary time: They prepared a person to react quickly to immediate physical danger in ways commonly referred to as *fight or flight*. Today, we have the same physiological responses to other, less immediately dangerous stressors. For example, driving in rush-hour traffic can result in the same responses as being faced by a wild bull (e.g., increased heartbeat, shortening of breath) (Kirsta, 1986).

When these physiological reactions occur often in someone who has not learned how to cope with them, they can result in a variety of unpleasant effects. You can reduce those effects by learning to care for yourself in ways that minimize or prevent negative reactions to stress. In general, you need to be able to do the following:

1. Find out whether you are exhibiting any of the typical negative effects of stress.
2. Identify possible causes of any negative stress symptoms you have.
3. Learn how to change yourself and/or your environment in ways that will reduce or eliminate your negative stress symptoms. You may not always be able to change external causes of stress, but you can change how you manage them (Kabat-Zinn, 1990).

The likely long-term negative result of stress is physical illness. Some of the illnesses or physical problems that can be induced or aggravated by stress reactions are as follows:

- Acne
- Alcoholism
- Allergies
- Asthma
- Colitis
- Constipation
- Dermatitis and eczema
- Diabetes
- Diarrhea
- Drug addiction
- Fatigue
- Headaches
- Heart conditions
- Insomnia
- Obesity
- Peptic ulcers
- Reduced interest in sex
- Rheumatoid arthritis
- Sexual dysfunction

(Greenberg & Valletutti, 1980; Turkington, 1998)

Fortunately, there are a host of physical, cognitive, and emotional warning signs that appear before one becomes seriously ill in response to stress. Different people display different warning signals: You may not have the same symptoms as the person in the next office, who has an ulcer, but you still may be at risk for physical illness. Typical physical warning signs of negative stress reactions are as follows:

- Alcohol or substance dependence
- Diarrhea, indigestion, vomiting
- Dry throat and mouth
- Excessive weight change
- Excessive nervous energy
- Fatigue
- Fainting
- Headaches
- High blood pressure

- Impulsive eating
- Muscle spasms
- Nausea
- Pain in back, neck, chest
- Sexual dysfunction
- Shortness of breath
- Sleeplessness
- Stuttering
- Sweating
- Teeth grinding
- Trembling

(Greenberg & Valletutti, 1980; Turkington, 1998)

Typical emotional, cognitive, or behavioral signs of negative stress reactions are as follows:

- Anxiety
- Apprehension about approaching weekends and vacations
- Constant uneasiness
- Depression
- Emotional outbursts (e.g., sobbing, temper tantrums)
- Feelings of rejection
- Feelings of failure
- Frustration
- General boredom
- General irritability

- Guilt
- Habitual or suppressed anger
- Helplessness
- Impulsive behavior
- Inability to concentrate
- Inability to have positive feelings
- Inability to laugh
- Irrational fears
- Lack of control
- Nightmares
- Recurring sense of hopelessness

(adapted from Andresen, 1995, and Greenberg & Valletutti, 1980)

If you have any of these physical or emotional signs of a negative stress reaction for a prolonged period of time, then consult your primary care physician. In addition, you may wish to consult a mental health professional for assistance in developing stress management skills. Any behavior that indicates you are not acting like yourself may be an adverse reaction to stress. Consistently acting out of character is a serious warning sign of decreased ability to cope and should not be ignored (Kirsta, 1986).

CHANGE AND STRESS

We burn out not because we don't care but because we don't grieve. We burn out because we have allowed our hearts to become so filled with loss that we have no room left to care.

(Remen, 1996, p. 52)

Johnn Young

I see people I haven't seen in years walk through those doors [at the AIDS clinic]. I see people who were very good friends walk through that door. I had a friend who passed away recently who was a client here. So I think I'm running out of time, and it saddens me to know that since I've been doing this, there's probably been about a dozen people who have passed away who I knew on a personal basis. It saddens you, it definitely saddens you.

Change at work appears to have reached epidemic proportions. Mergers, downsizing, and managed health care are some of the major catalysts for the workplace changes encountered by human services professionals. People often resist change because it brings or appears to bring a loss of control or a shift in power, or it brings a fear of not having skills needed in the changed workplace (Kaye, 1997). Grief reactions to change are almost universal: People may feel grief over losses, threatened losses, or what they have never had (Jeffreys, 1995). Common grief reactions include anger; pain; shame; fear; and guilt, including survivor guilt felt by those who still have jobs when others have been laid off (Jeffreys, 1995). Grief can't be ignored: Going through the emotional process is essential to healing (Bridges, 1988) and generally takes longer than anyone wishes. Consequently, being aware of your cognitive and emotional reactions to changes at work is an essential first step in coping with change.

Suzanne Cardiff

There's always laws changing, rules changing, agency policies changing. Clients change from day to day, cases change, co-workers change. It's just constant change—just when you think you have it down. Don't relax. If you love variety, you don't like the same thing day after day? Perfect job. I've seen so many case workers, they come in, they're so relaxed, oh my cases are going so well, nothing's going wrong. [The] next phone call comes—forget that line!

Heidi Daly

Coping with change, boy that's a tough one. Probably the biggest challenge is when staff changes, especially people that you work closely with, because you have to really get to know the person and see how they do things and change how you approach them.

Jennifer Echarte

When Medicaid capitation made them cut my job from the mental health center, I got moved over to adolescent treatment. I sort of looked at it positively, because I'm going to have a whole new experience, and I get to know the system better. This for me is education before I go back to school to specialize. So, the change is something that excites me, but we've got to move offices. Some people are not going to return to their jobs, so everybody's constantly fearing a loss of their job. Every year there is a threat, and every year there's a cut. It's part of working for the mental health center. It would be nice to have some job security and to feel better about the place you're working, that they're not just gonna lay you off.

William Esp

It's very, very hard coping with change. There's been countless times when initially I just dug my heels in, saying, "This is gonna be horrible, this is gonna be terrible, this is gonna be awful," only to find out that actually it freshened things up and kept things going. So, I try to always remind myself whenever changes come along that maybe there'll be some good—usually I can find some. My sense is the people who don't change burn out.

That's the beauty of change: It's what's so much fun some days and sometimes really scary, waiting to see what's around the corner, waiting to see what the next day brings. A lot of that's my own recovery and a lot of that's my work, which in some ways are really inseparable.

Christa Pavlus

It was very hard for me to learn to give myself a little bit of distance. I became so attached to people, and especially working in geriatrics you tend to lose a lot of the people you work with. I internalized everything, and I felt everything so totally and fully that it was very hard for me to remember my professionalism and also learn that I can't save the world. I can sure help it as much as I can, but I can't save the world. It's a difficult thing to learn to step back a little bit. I think I'm getting pretty good at that.

Ellen Berlin

We have to keep looking to change because otherwise there is going to be a point that, because we aren't a money-making program, that they're gonna say, we love you, you've been good, [but] see you around. So somehow you have to keep up.

Johnn Young

I have just decided, after hitting my 43rd birthday, that change is a constant and things are going to always change. I know that right now the work I have to do will change in probably 30 seconds; something else has jumped to the top of the list. As long as I know change is a constant, then I'm going to be okay with it, and that's how I deal with it. Even things that have no life to them like rocks change. It's amazing when you finally realize that, when you finally get it.

STRESS MANAGEMENT THROUGH SELF-CARE

When you are raised to be perpetually nice, to fail to do so feels like being mean.
                                        (Singleton, 1993a, p. 7B)

People who work in human services spend much of their time meeting the needs of others. Sometimes we feel guilty about taking the time and energy to care for ourselves. Sometimes we are accused of being selfish when we do take care of ourselves. The implied message is that it is not possible to care for others *and* care for ourselves. That is a dangerous message. *Self-care is not selfish!* People who behave selfishly do not take others into account. People who are self-caring recognize that all people are valuable and that they are just as entitled to be self-caring as anyone else. People who care for themselves are much more likely to be good at their jobs than people who ignore their personal needs. In the long run we are not going to do the best job or be the best friends or partners or parents we can be when we neglect ourselves.

The best way to manage stress and prevent burnout is to treat yourself well, to take the time to care for yourself. That means being able to recognize your needs and how to meet them. A good place to start is by asking yourself what is important to you. Possible categories might include personal (health, intellect, emotion), family, friends, community, country, humanity, planet.

Suzanne Cardiff

The winter is really busy. A lot of people get stressed out more in the winter than in the summer 'cause there are less ways to let it out. Most people are sun people—they need to be outdoors in the sun, and that makes them feel better. In the winter people get depressed. So, stress management is a huge thing. I find I just do the best I can, and when I get a break I take it. I don't give it up for anything. It's impossible in this job to always just go home and punch yourself out of the clock, especially when you have friends who you work with and hang out with you on the weekends. You always end up talking about cases, and you go, "Hey, we're not supposed to be talking about work." We'll get all stressed out and ruin the whole weekend.

Ellen Berlin

Sometimes in this field you just get tired of listening. It's just sometimes you get so full, and then I think we need therapists, we need our own support groups. There's ways we try to do that at work, but not enough.

You have to find boundaries for yourself. I just read Kushner's book, *How Good Do We Have to Be?* and that has reenergized my personal and professional life. I think as I get older, I feel like I'm finding a better balance. I spend many hours in the summer and the fall and the spring on my bicycle, and it's regrown who I am. It's how I've balanced more.

I teach a class on stress—it's a wonder I haven't learned how to manage it yet. I'm learning as I go. To put it into your actions, into your own life so you can remain emotionally and mentally healthy is survival. I laugh at that all the time. I talk about discipline and teach it, then go home and [try to] live it. Our youngest gets into the car after school, and he hasn't done anything all day. I've just come from a parenting class where we talked about setting limits and responsibility and letting them feel the pain, and I say everything I know shouldn't be coming out of my mouth. That keeps you on your toes.

I wish that I could have figured out a way to get better support for myself all along the way.

Exercises

8-1. List what is important to you in all aspects of your life.
8-2. List how you currently meet your needs in each of those areas.
8-3. Identify the areas in which you would like to improve your self-care.

Pamela Meister

It's interesting that although I'm dealing with more people in a crisis situation in this job, the stress is much less for me than when I was in sales. Take Friday afternoon: I had three different people who were medically indigent, one who actually tried to attack me. That's the first time that happened, and I was stressed. However, I can leave it here and go, "Well, I feel good about what I accomplished." When I was in sales, I would end the day, but I was still going, "Okay, how am I going to increase sales for this month? My job's in jeopardy if I don't meet quota." Because that didn't always fit with my own values, there was more stress.

Cathy Phelps

One of the things that I added to annual performance evaluations for everybody I supervise is a self-care evaluation. The first couple months of the year, the staff write out goals and objectives for how they're going to take care of themselves during the year, and part of supervision is checking in with that. It could be something as basic as taking a time management class, exercising, taking a yoga class, reading a number of books, starting a book group, or signing up for a class that they've wanted to take. Some of the other interesting things people have done: getting into graduate school and getting a baby sitter once a month so a woman and her partner can go out. They love it, they enjoy it, and they take it seriously. Taking care of themselves becomes something they really enjoy. I try to do it by doing different things professionally and by placing value on having a personal life.

Johnn Young

I've just learned to take time for myself. I don't eat in my office anymore. I take classes on stress management because you tend to forget, you tend to get so busy you forget. If I didn't do the stress management, if I didn't take the time to spend time with my partner and spend time with friends and things like that, I would not be a happy camper. If I'm miserable, everybody around me is miserable, because I'm going to share.

I've gotten very good at balancing personal and professional. I'm on the board of directors of an organization called Out for Life. Its purpose is to do HIV prevention in the community of people of African descent. Since it's a new organization, I will get calls at home from people on the board. I finally had to get to the point where I said I'd love to talk to you at home about your personal lives and my life, and I'd love to talk to you at work about professional life, and that's how I have to do it. I also have a partner who will remind me, "Johnn, we are out at dinner, can we talk about something besides what you do for a living?" Occasionally people will come to talk to me when I'm out, and I will tell people, "I am out to have a good time, do you want to make an appointment and come by my office?" Some people get offended when they want your time on demand. I just have to set boundaries, I have to say this is [not] work, this is professional and keep very clear about [separating] the two, which is hard.

Right now you may not have any negative reactions to stress, either because there is not a great deal of tension in your life or because you have developed good stress management skills. If you are feeling fine, then you may wonder if there is any reason to bother reading this chapter. There is a good reason: When you are doing well is the best time to 1) review what you are doing well and 2) identify any new self-care skills you may want to acquire.

DEVELOPING A SELF-CARE PLAN

This section is about improving your self-care skills and therefore improving your ability to manage stress. No one has exactly the same needs for self-care, so no two plans will be alike. Thus, this chapter does not provide you with a list of things you should do to care for yourself. Instead, the following are provided: 1) a general strategy for developing a self-care plan that fits you and 2) a discussion of tactics some people find useful.

You are likely to be more successful at self-care when you use the following guidelines.

- *Start small.* We are all familiar with the person who makes a resolution to start the new year off by making a major improvement in her life but never carries it through. That is because real, permanent change does not occur in dramatic ways; instead, it occurs in a series of small, manageable steps that are taken one at a time (Jaffe & Scott, 1984). For instance, a major career change might start with updating your résumé.

- *Do something now.* Change in how you manage stress, as with any other change, requires action; merely thinking about change is not enough (and doing so may increase the stress in your life). Your first attempt may not be successful, but you will have begun the habit of actively working to care for yourself more effectively. Examples of beginning attempts to improve self-care include taking 5 minutes for yourself when you first get home from work, reading for 10 minutes every day during your lunch break, and closing the door to your office for 5 minutes of daydreaming time.

- *Set clear, specific goals.* As Sachs (1998) recommended, it is helpful to set clear, specific goals for yourself. For instance, you might decide your goal is to walk for 10 minutes during your lunch break at least three times a week, starting next Monday.

- *Set proactive goals.* You may want to stop blaming yourself, stop losing your temper, or stop trying to control everything, but you will not be successful unless you learn what to do in place of these behaviors (Bernstein et al., 1981). Things to do might include the following: 1) analyzing what happened when things have gone wrong and learning from your analysis instead of blaming yourself; 2) taking a deep breath and counting to 10 so that you control your temper when you feel yourself starting to get angry; or 3) identifying at least one thing at work every day that you cannot control and saying to yourself, "I can't do anything about that, and it's okay that I can't control it."

- *Set meaningful goals.* Set goals that are meaningful and important to you, not goals you think you "should" set or that others tell you to set. If you start working with what is most important to you, then you will be taking advantage of your strongest motivation for change.

- *Be selective.* Be clear about your priorities and focus on what is most important to you.

- *Start from where you are, not from where you want to be.* Suppose your long-term goal is to engage in aerobic exercise a minimum of six times a week for at least 45 minutes each time, but currently you are not exercising at all. Start by comparing your progress with where you have been, not where you want to go. A week in which you exercised 20 minutes for 3 days is not good when you compare it with your long-term goal, but it is terrific when you compare it with your starting point!

• *Make changes one at a time.* It is generally easier to make one change at a time (Sachs, 1998). Do not, for example, try to quit smoking, go on a diet, and quit drinking all at the same time.

• *Plan ahead.* If part of your plan is to spend more time with supportive friends who have very busy schedules, then make arrangements with them to go to dinner or a movie instead of waiting until the last minute and finding everyone busy.

• *Make it easy.* For instance, it may be easier to exercise in a health club by yourself than to try to schedule a handball court and partner. Or, it may be even easier to buy an exercise bike and work out at home.

• *Reward yourself for doing good work and caring for yourself.* Plan the reward you will give yourself when you complete an important project. Make signs, graphs, or public announcements each time you complete another step in a larger project. Also, remind yourself of all the things you are doing to take care of yourself.

• *Pick techniques likely to work for you.* If you dislike traveling in hot weather, then plan winter vacations. If large parties are events you wish to avoid, then plan social evenings with small groups of friends.

• *Look for ways to take control of your life.* Rearrange the furniture in your office, sit in a new place at a regular meeting, or decide when you want to return a call. There are many ways you can control your life. This does not mean you will be getting rid of spontaneity. It means you will be structuring your life in ways that work for you. For instance, you may decide to do household chores on weeknights so that Saturdays can be unstructured.

• *Do it every day: New skills require constant practice* (Forman & Cecil, 1985). The more often you have reacted to stress in ways that makes matters worse, the more likely you are to react in the same ways in the future. Thus, daily practice is necessary to learn a new self-care skill well enough so that it will replace your old, dysfunctional reactions to stress. You may want to keep a card on your desk or in a pocket so that you can make a tally mark every time you practice your new skill. This can help remind you to practice and can show you your progress.

• *Be patient and persistent.* Your first attempts will not always be successful. Learn from them, and try something different.

• *Finally, reassess your self-care skills and your need for them regularly.* Whenever there is any sort of major change in your life, sources of stress are likely to change. Some of the changes will cause less stress, others will cause more.

Heidi Daly

You're going to have stress. You will have stress. Trying to figure out what is causing the stress and how to avoid that or, if you cannot avoid it, how to lessen it, I'm not very good at it. My stress management is not very good at all. To know how you react to stress is a big way of coping with it. I can guarantee when I was first in social work, I definitely internalized it, and that's part of the reason why I had such trouble in working with it and dealing with it.

You have to give yourself time away and give yourself relaxation time. Let yourself be around other people who aren't even in the business. Don't talk about it [your work] all the time— you will if you are around it all the time.

TOPICS TO ADDRESS IN SELF-CARE PLANS

Everone has a unique combination of self-care needs. The rest of this chapter discusses causes and ways of managing stress as it relates to your physical and mental well-being, your environment, work, and support systems. These are some of the many ways you may choose to care for yourself. Stress as a positive force is also addressed.

PHYSICAL WELL-BEING

In general, the better you are at taking care of your body, the less stressed you will feel. The reason for this is simple: If you feel good physically, then you will be better able to respond to sources of stress in your life. If you do not feel good, then your ability to respond effectively to stressful situations will be impaired. For instance, most of us have experienced the effects that a headache or lack of sleep can have on productivity and tolerance.

Strategies for Maintaining Good Physical Health

Nearly everyone knows good health depends on eating well, exercising regularly, having routine checkups, and relaxing regularly. Knowing what to do, however, does not automatically lead to doing it. Briefly, here are the four building blocks for maintaining and/or improving your physical well-being.

Eat Well, and Eat At Least Three Meals a Day   There are four food elements that are particularly likely to interfere with your ability to manage stress: caffeine, sugar, salt, and alcohol. These are often called *mood foods* because they can have a significant effect on your mood and, thus, on your ability to stay calm under stress (Kirsta, 1986). Caffeine has a "speed" effect, and too much of it can make you jumpy and irritable. Sugar leads to a quick high followed by a quick low. Too much salt will lead to excessive water retention and a bloated feeling. Alcohol can act temporarily as a stimulant but will act as a powerful depressant with continued consumption (Kirsta, 1986).

The less you use these four foods and the more you eat a balanced diet, the better you will feel and the more able you will be to cope with daily stress (for more specifics on eating well, see Brody, 1990).

Exercise Regularly   There are three components to physical fitness: flexibility, strength, and cardiovascular endurance. Two common ways to develop flexibility are through yoga or stretching exercises. Strength can result from activities such as weight lifting, use of weight training equipment, or calisthenics. Aerobic exercise such as aerobic dance, running, swimming, walking, or bicycle riding are needed for cardiovascular fitness. Consistent practice in one of the martial arts such as tai chi can improve one or more fitness components. Do remember to increase the amount you exercise gradually and to consult your physician before beginning a new exercise program.

The most important aspect of any fitness plan is consistency: No exercise will be effective unless you do it regularly. One useful way to encourage yourself to exercise regularly is to set a regular appointment with yourself to exercise and keep it as faithfully as you would mealtimes, bathing, or a date with a friend.

Have Regular Checkups   Many physical illnesses can be treated and cured when they are identified early. Checkups will help determine whether a symptom such as extreme fatigue is caused by a physical disorder that can be treated medically.

> *Discipline does not disappear forever, but she does take*
> *vacations from time to time.*
> *(Gendler, 1984, p. 11)*

> *[Justice Louis] Brandeis was once criticized for taking a*
> *short vacation just before the start of an important trial. "I*
> *need the rest," explained Brandeis. "I find that I can do a*
> *year's work in eleven months, but I can't do it in twelve."*
> *(Fadiman, 1985, p. 76)*

Relax Regularly   Many people find it difficult to relax, both physically and emotionally. They may not have taken the time and learned the skills to relax physically. They may have so much to occupy their thoughts that they never stop trying to solve problems, regardless of whether the problems are professional or personal. Failure to relax increases the stress one feels, both mentally and physically.

When you are very busy with work, it is easy to forget to take time to relax or even to forget how to relax. Formal approaches to relaxing and stepping back from daily pressures can be useful ways to interrupt this cycle. Some people meditate daily. Others use a technique called *progressive muscle relaxation* (Auerbach & Gramling, 1998; Bernstein & Borkovec, 1973).

Progressive muscle relaxation can be an important tool because it helps you to substitute a relaxation response for tension in your body. The training involves learning to tense and relax various muscle groups while learning to tell the difference between how tension feels and how relaxation feels. Many of us do not have the ability to distinguish between tension and relaxation in our own bodies. Initial training in this technique is usually conducted by a skilled trainer, often a trained therapist. The person practices the tensing and relaxing sequence at home and/or at work, often with the aid of an audiocassette with recorded instructions. Next, relaxing the sequence of muscles is practiced without tensing first. Finally, the person learns to associate the feeling of deep relaxation with a verbal cue such as the word "calm" (Forman & Cecil, 1985). Progressive muscle relaxation can be a powerful aid to regular relaxing. It is not, however, a skill you can easily teach yourself. If you are interested, find a trainer. Often, they are associated with health maintenance organizations or behavior therapy groups.

There are a myriad of other ways of relaxing. Different strategies work for different people, and the amount and type of relaxation one needs vary from person to person. Many people think of taking a vacation as their primary way to relax, particularly when the vacation consists of sitting in a boat, holding a fishing rod, or doing some other similarly slow-paced, unpressured activity. Although longer vacations of 1 or 2 weeks are the norm, some people find several 4- or 5-day vacations throughout the year more relaxing than one long break. Vacations are often relaxing, but sometimes they can be a source of stress. This is particularly likely to happen when you try to take a vacation you cannot afford, when people spending vacation time with you have different expectations than yours about what is going to happen, or when you try to do too much in too short a time. Also, because vacations occur infrequently, they are not a substitute for learning to incorporate relaxation strategies into our daily lives.

People such as human services workers whose work is largely verbal and not physical often relax by working with their hands. Gardening, woodworking, and cooking, all of which have tangible outcomes, are popular examples. That is because it can be difficult to identify the outcomes of working with people and equally difficult to figure out who is responsible for which outcomes. Human services workers sometimes are not able to point to a concrete outcome and say, "I did that."

Exercise

8-4.   Consider how well you take care of yourself physically.
    a.   What are your best stress management skills with respect to your physical health?
    b.   What stress management skills would you like to improve with respect to your physical health?

YOUR PHYSICAL ENVIRONMENT

We interact with the world around us through our senses. Although no one has complete control over sensory input, most of us have some ability to manage what we hear, see, smell, and feel. Because the sight, sound, smell, and feel of your physical environment can increase or reduce stress levels, one useful way to care for yourself and prevent negative reactions to stress is to manage your physical environment. Here are some of the ways people make their physical environments more comfortable, both at home and at work:

1.   *Sight.* Hang pictures or other things you like to look at on the walls. Paint the walls or furniture a pleasing color. Put something you like to look at on your desk. Arrange things in your home or office in ways you find appealing. Make the lighting as pleasant and easy on your eyes as possible.
2.   *Sound.* Play music you find relaxing or calming, shut your door to avoid unpleasant sounds, or hang drapes to absorb sound. If you share a large open office that is noisy, wear ear plugs when you want to concentrate.
3.   *Smell.* Fight pollution by keeping houseplants, flowers, bowls of water, humidifiers, and/or air cleaners in your office. If you are a nonsmoker, then ask people to refrain from smoking in your office.
4.   *Touch.* Obtain comfortable furniture, particularly your office chair. Many people find chairs designed especially for back comfort important. If you use a computer, make sure that your keyboard, monitor, computer desk, and chair are arranged to prevent repetitive strain injuries. Get a footrest if you need one to sit comfortably at your desk or computer.

Exercise

8-5.   Consider how well you take care of yourself with respect to
       your physical environment.
       a.   How does your physical environment help you man-
            age stress?
       b.   How would you like to improve your physical environ-
            ment?

Jennifer Echarte

It's a little bit difficult for me, because I don't have an office. Having an office is so key to this work, because you can
leave your work there and come home, but I end up doing paperwork at home, making calls from home, doing things at home
so there is a constant mixing. There is a main office where I can
go and make calls if I want to, but I don't have my own desk and
I don't have my own phone. You can work in the kitchen, or you
can work in a conference room, but you don't know when
there's going to be a conference. So my office is my car.

THOUGHTS AND STRESS

Worry has written the definitive work on nervous habits. . . .

*Guilt is the prosecutor who knows how to make every vic-
tim feel like the criminal.*
                                        (Gendler, 1984, pp. 3, 25)

Stress is often self-created. Remember, stress is our reaction to the
demands placed on us. Sometimes we create negative stress for ourselves by not taking care of our bodies. Sometimes we create negative
stress for ourselves by repeating thoughts that are irrational and counterproductive. Below you will find a list of common irrational
thoughts. Dr. Rian McMullin (1987) compiled this list primarily from
surveys and clinical observations made by dozens of therapists, guid-
ance counselors, special educators, psychiatric nurses, social workers,
and other mental health specialists. McMullin also took items from
Ellis and Harper's (1976) *A New Guide to Rational Living* and Hauck's
(1967) *The Rational Management of Children*. The following thoughts are
not irrational under all circumstances, but they often occur under conditions that make them irrational.

Common Irrational Thoughts

- People must always love me, or I will be miserable.
- Making mistakes is terrible.
- It is terrible when things go wrong.
- I should not feel the way I feel.
- My emotions can't be controlled.
- Self-discipline is too hard to achieve.
- I must always depend on others.
- My childhood will always dominate my behavior as an adult.
- I believe there is a single perfect solution for my problem, and all I have to do is find it.
- I am an exceptional person (prince or superwoman in disguise) and require special privileges and favors. I shouldn't have to live within the limits and restrictions of ordinary mortals.
- Beliefs held by respected authorities or society must be correct and therefore shouldn't be questioned.
- A good human services professional would not have made that mistake.
- If others criticize me, then I must have done something wrong.
- I can't help what I think. If I think there is something wrong with me, then there is.
- To be a good, moral, worthwhile person, I must help everyone who needs it. (Many mental health specialists said they believed this at the beginning of their careers.)
- To be a manly man or a feminine woman, my sexual performance must always be outstanding, every time with every partner. Any inability to do so means I am a failure or a homosexual. (Ellis and other sex therapists reported that many clients have this thought.)
- If I ever get anxious, fearful, or depressed, then I very likely will go crazy.
- There is one true love, and the person I am dating is it for me. If he ever leaves me, then I might as well pack it in. (Counselors in college counseling centers reported that many students think this.)
- I ought to and must solve my problems quickly and without a great deal of effort.
- It is the therapist's responsibility to solve my problems. She's the doctor, isn't she? You cure me, and I'll sit here and watch. (More than 20 therapists reported this one.)
- Strong, healthy, stable people solve their own problems. If you ask for help, then you are weak, sick, or a coward.
- If I don't want to do something, then I can't do it. I just have to wait around until the mood hits me before I can take action. (Counselors

helping students improve their study habits noted that students often had this thought.)

- If something is possible, then it is likely to happen.
- The whole community is watching what I am doing. They are evaluating how well I do.
- Before I make a decision, I must have a guarantee that it is the right one.
- I have to get it right the first time I do it.
- I should be like others.
- People shouldn't try to change their thoughts or feelings because they are natural and genuine to them.
- In order to solve my problems, I must know the exact origin of them.
- I should get very angry when people don't trust me, even when they don't know me.
- I should feel happy and contented all the time.
- I have a secret, hidden self inside of me that is sinister and could explode.
- Working to solve my problems is more dangerous than doing nothing.
- It's unfair that the world is not the way I would like it to be.
- I am not responsible for what happens to me. Others are at fault when things go wrong for me.
- I must control my anxiety constantly. Otherwise, it will overcome me and make me into a psychotic or cause me to do insane things.
- I won't listen to therapists because there is absolutely nothing they can tell me about myself that I don't already know.
- I can't accept myself unless I have self-confidence.
- I have never lived up to my potential.
- I am unlucky.
- When I trust people, they always seem to let me down.
- I should be different from what I am.
- I am a born worrier.
- If you really get to know me, then you won't like me.
- I can always tell what people think of me.
- Happy people have free, uncontrolled emotions.
- How bad I feel about losing someone shows how much I cared for her.
- The stronger I feel something, the more likely it's true.

(From McMullin, R.C. [1987]. *Talk sense to yourself: A guide to cognitive restructuring therapies.* Adapted by permission of the Institute for Rational Emotive Psychotherapy.)

William Esp

Probably the other thing, and I learned this in my recovery, is humility. It's not that I don't have responsibility, but I'm not responsible for whether a person makes it or not. I've seen so many professionals just go nuts, because they really believe that they have the power to affect the overall outcome. We influence for sure, but I don't do this, the client does the work. I'm just here for the ride. I always thank clients for letting me be part of the experience when they make it—that is why I do the work. I'm not the be all and the end all. People burn out immediately, I think, when they put themselves in that position.

We create stress for ourselves when we rehearse and endorse irrational and counterproductive thoughts such as the ones listed previously. The way to stop yourself from perpetuating this useless pattern is to learn to think differently about difficulties. Three strategies you can use to help you cope with irrational thoughts are as follows: counters, limiting when and where you worry, and thought-stopping.

Counters

Counters are alternatives to the irrational thoughts that you create. For example, suppose that you often have the following irrational thought, "To be a good, moral, worthwhile person, I must help everyone who needs it." A counter to this would be "I'm only one person, and it's okay if I do a good job of helping a few people. It's silly to think I can be a superperson and help everyone."

Here is a second example of a counter. Suppose your supervisor calls you into her office and tells you that although your work with people is very good, your reports are not as clearly written as they should be. She then gives you several examples of how to improve and offers to review and comment on draft versions of your reports. Here are some irrational thoughts that might make this situation worse:

- Boy, I've really screwed it up this time.
- She must think I'm pretty stupid.
- I'll never get a good letter of recommendation now.
- I'm just doing a terrible job.
- Nothing I can do pleases her.

Suppose you find yourself repeating this sequence of thoughts and are feeling worse with each repetition. Consider the first thought in the previous list: "I've really screwed it up this time." This thought may be true, but it is unlikely to make you feel better. A good question to ask yourself is "What do I need to do to help myself feel better?" You may decide that what will make you feel better is figuring out how to improve and thus avoid negative feedback in the future. What might you want to tell yourself instead? Here is one set of possible counters:

Boy, I've really screwed it up this time. . . .
- But she did tell me what I do well.
- I guess I need to do something about my report writing.
- Well, she showed me how to improve.
- I will set aside a little time every day to practice my reports. Today I have 30 minutes free, from 2:00 till 2:30, so I'll practice then.
- It's good to have a supervisor who will help me improve.

If you have a small number of irrational thoughts that bother you frequently, then you may find it useful to write down your counters and keep them in a place where you can refer to them often (Ellis & Harper, 1976).

Many irrational thoughts are related to guilt. One way to define *guilt* is as a combination of a thought about what you think you should have done or not done combined with a negative feeling (Kubany & Manke, 1995). For example, you might think, "I should have done a better job for that client," and feel sad and frustrated. A more useful way to think about past mistakes is "I wish I had handled that situation differently, but I can't change the past. I will try to change in the future." This is a more useful approach because it emphasizes what is possible instead of something you cannot change.

Limit When and Where You Worry

Most of us worry some of the time, and sometimes with good reason. However, worrying too often and in the wrong places can give us even more to fret about if we worry instead of working. Because it is unrealistic to plan to stop worrying altogether, an alternative strategy is to limit your worrying to only certain times and a limited number of places. For instance, you might decide to allow yourself to worry about what your supervisor thinks of you only during your morning coffee break. Even better, you might also decide that, during the times you are allowed to worry, you must also think about how to improve so you will not have as much to worry about. Finally, an important part of this strategy is that you do not allow yourself to worry about your supervisor's opinion of you at any other time.

Thought-Stopping

Thought-stopping is just what it sounds like. You tell yourself loudly and definitely to "Stop!" thinking an irrational thought. Thought-stopping is particularly useful at times when you should be concentrating on something else and do not have time to come up with counters. An important meeting is an example of a time when you might want to use thought-stopping.

Exercises

8-6.   Consider how well you take care of yourself with respect to your thoughts.
   a.   What are your effective skills at managing irrational thoughts?
   b.   What skills at managing irrational thoughts would you like to improve?
8-7.   Pick two irrational thoughts from the list above that you have regularly. For each one, write out at least two counters.
8-8.   Plan two ways to use thought-stopping.

Suzanne Cardiff

Balancing personal and professional [concerns] is the same as stress management to me. You have to learn not to bring your personal into your professional life and vice versa, which is really hard. Sometimes you get so hung up on getting so involved in everyone's personal life that you forget and bring your own in. You have to remind yourself, "This is nobody's business but my own; I don't need to bring it to work." Sometimes you need to leave your "social worker shoes," I like to call them, at the office. You also can't go lecturing all your friends and everything on social worker standards.

STRESS AT WORK

When you find yourself reacting negatively to work-related stress, the problem may be with one or more of the following: 1) how you manage stress, 2) how the organization manages you, and 3) how much you are being asked to do. Here are some characteristics of an organization that is well-managed:

- It is clear to you what is expected of you (Greenberg & Valletutti, 1980).
- You have the authority to carry out your responsibilities (Greenberg & Valletutti, 1980).

- You have some role in planning your contribution to the organization. This does not mean complete control, but it does mean that you are included to some extent in the decision-making process (Greenberg & Valletutti, 1980).
- You get clear, regular feedback about what you have done well and what you need to do to improve.
- You are not asked to do more than is humanly possible or to act in ways that are not ethical.
- Self-care is encouraged and seen as a way to keep people healthy and productive.

Here are some of the things you can do to manage stress at work:

- If you are not clear about what is expected of you, then ask.
- Associate primarily with people who are willing to try to solve problems, not with people who complain loudly but do not try to solve anything (Greenberg & Valletutti, 1980).
- If you want more feedback, then ask for it.
- Do not try to do everything by yourself—if you need help, then ask for it.
- Learn your limits and do not take on more than you can competently handle.
- Have fun at your job. Just because you do serious work does not mean you have to be serious all the time.
- Look for another job when the one you have is not healthy for you. For instance, a mismatch between your job requirements and job qualifications may be related to increased dissatisfaction with your work (Hromco, Lyons, & Nikkel, 1995). Also, an organization that expects you to do wonderful things for others but does not support self-care is not a healthy place to work. (See Chapter 7 for information on looking for a job.)

> *If you are in trouble and your management asks you to work harder without offering anything different to do, anything that seems to have a hopeful wisdom to it, float your résumé. This [organization] is a sinking ship.*
> *(Cowan, 1992, p. 120)*

Exercise

8-9. Consider how well you take care of yourself at work.
   a. Identify your best self-care skills with respect to your work.
   b. What would you like to improve?

SUPPORT SYSTEMS

Ellen Berlin

Childbirth educators have meetings—I usually don't go because my other job doesn't allow that. [The meetings] let you get the support you need just connecting with other childbirth educators. In the parent education job, as a department we've plugged in one Friday every month for support group to lessen stress because many of us have only 1 day or 2 that we're even in the office together—we're all teaching different classes in the community—and we really need support because we hear a lot about a lot of people's lives. So, to try to make that happen, we've said last Friday of every month, this is gonna happen, and it's helped a little in our department.

Most people choose to live and work with other people rather than in isolation. They desire the company and support of others. This section is about support: what it is and where one usually finds it.

Often, when *support* is mentioned, it is interpreted as *emotional support*. In fact, there are many forms of support, including the following: 1) listening, 2) appreciation for our skills, 3) challenges to improve our skills, 4) emotional support, 5) reality testing (Gardner & Chapman, 1985), 6) challenges to work harder (Jaffe & Scott, 1984), and 7) technical assistance.

Each of us has a unique set of individual needs for support in terms of what type of support we need, which people can provide it, and how many of them we look to for support. Also, each of us has different skills at providing various types of support for others.

Support comes from a variety of sources. Most of us have different organizations and people to whom we turn for different forms of support. The most common sources are 1) intimate relationships (spouses, partners), 2) family members, 3) friends, 4) colleagues, 5) members of professional organizations, 6) members of community organizations, and 7) people in support groups (Jaffe & Scott, 1984).

If you are going to manage the stress in your life successfully, you will need to know what types of support work for you and where to find them, as well as what kind of support you can give, and to whom. Following are some ways to improve your support systems:

- Identify the people whose support is most important to you, and tell them how much you appreciate their support.
- Plan your time so that as much of it as possible is spent with people who are supportive.

- Ask for the support you need.
- Give support to others.
- Decrease time spent with people who are not supportive.

(adapted from Jaffe & Scott, 1984)

Exercises

8-10.   What kinds of support do you need? Rank the seven types of support described previously in order of importance to you.
8-11.   List at least one person from whom you get each type of support.
8-12.   List three activities you enjoy that will improve your support systems (e.g., meeting new people, spending more time with people you care about). Implement these activities.

STRESS AS A POSITIVE FORCE

Stress can be a positive experience. Many of our responses to the demands placed on us are positive and are healthy for us physically and/or mentally. Often new challenges make us feel excited and glad to be alive. Although this chapter has emphasized coping with negative stress reactions, please remember that some stress is healthy: Only when you cannot cope effectively with the demands placed on you does stress become negative.

Following are additional methods people use to take care of themselves:

- Get involved in a creative experience. Take up a craft, sing in a chorus, or write poetry.
- Spend time with people who do not work in human services. If you spend all of your nonwork time with people who do human services work, then you may forget that there are other ways of looking at the world. Exposure to a variety of people and ideas can be an exciting way of relaxing and refreshing yourself.
- Spend some time alone. Although individual tolerance levels differ, few of us want to spend every minute of our waking hours with other people.
- Do something for someone else that has no connection with your work. Many people find personal fulfillment in volunteer work; human services professionals often do. Some of us do volunteer work

related to human services, such as serving as a board member or helping with special recreational activities. Others prefer to volunteer in different ways, by doing things such as working on political campaigns, volunteering in animal shelters, or supporting the arts.

- Laugh a lot. The human condition can be painful and funny at the same time.

William Esp

Actually I think stress management is one area I do really well in. The vast majority of the time I find by the time I'm two or three blocks away in my truck, I'm already at home and able to separate. I think one of the things that helps is I have a pretty diverse life. I'm a musician, and I play in a blues band. I'm out there, and it's antithetical to my work, and actually I love that. I love just going where nobody talks about clients or patients. That's why the music is so important to me. And then having stuff from my spiritual practice. I've been part of a men's council for years and years and years. There's just so many things that keep me healthy.

I'm also into indigenous drumming. A lot of times if I've had a really stressful group and I feel like I'm maybe taking some of that toxic stuff home with me, I'll use sage, and I'll drum for 20 minutes, half an hour when I get home. I find that it really alleviates a lot of that stress.

Exercises

8-12. Make a list of the things you already do for your personal growth, and make a second list of the things you would like to begin doing for your personal growth.

8-13. Pick two changes you want to make in your life that will contribute to your personal growth. Make plans for how you are going to make each change. Start implementing one of the plans. Set a time to evaluate whether it is helping you. Start implementing the second plan when you feel ready to add that change to your life.

DIANA AND FRIENDS DISCUSS STRESS

"Hey, this chapter was great! It gave me permission to take care of me," Akram tells the group. "When I really sat down and thought about it, I realized the only way to take care of myself is to start looking for another job. I know every agency has too much to do, but I need to find one that has more realistic expectations of staff. I've started updating my résumé."

"Good for you!" Diana tells him. "My self-care plan is a little less dramatic. Work is going better, but I need to do more for myself outside of work. I've wanted to learn to paint watercolors for a long time, so I signed up for a class that starts next week."

"Okay, Hunter, your turn to report," Diana says.

Hunter says, "That section on thoughts and stress was an eye-opener. I've been stressing myself out by thinking about everything that can go wrong with the new structure at work. I hadn't considered the possibility that some of the changes might actually improve things. Now I'm trying to keep an open mind about what's going on. It's amazing how much better I feel since I started changing my thinking."

CHAPTER 9

The Proactive Human Services Professional
or
Putting It All Together

OBJECTIVE:

- Identify your long-term professional and personal development goals.

This book is about the search for answers to the following questions:

- What do I expect to get out of doing human services work?
- What do I expect to accomplish in my work?
- What will my values be as I provide services?
- How do I act while I provide services?
- How do I manage the stress of working in human services?

Each of the first eight chapters addresses one or more of these questions. This closing chapter is intended to bring those pieces together and leave you with a holistic picture of human services as a career.

HUMAN SERVICES AS A CAREER

Some people enter human services work intending to make it a career; others never planned such a long-term commitment—it just seemed to happen to them. If a large part of your life is to be spent working in one of the human services, then it is important to think of and approach your work as part of a professional career. This does *not* necessarily mean you must always be looking for the next career move or promotion, although you may wish to do so. It means you take your work seriously enough to plan for your own professional development in whatever way you choose. There is a myth that human services workers do not, and perhaps should not, think of themselves and their careers because they should be selfless people who dedicate their lives to others. This, in the author's opinion, is a dangerous myth. If you do not take yourself seriously, then you cannot be expected to take the people you serve seriously, and you cannot expect to be taken seriously as a human services professional.

One of the primary goals of this chapter is to convey what it takes to create a positive, fulfilling career in human services work. First, this chapter takes a broad look at how the careers of two human services professionals have developed over time. Next, you will hear once more from those professionals whose comments appear throughout this book. In closing, you will be asked to take one last look at your own professional development.

Reactions to interviews vary widely from person to person, so your friends and colleagues may get very different messages from the interviews than you do. For that reason you may find it helpful to discuss the interviews and your perspective on them with several other individuals.

PROFILE: CHERYL LAMMERS

Cheryl Lammers is a probation officer. She was 31 and had been a probation officer for $8\frac{1}{2}$ years when she was interviewed for the first edition. She was interviewed again for the second edition. Here are the answers she gave at both interviews.

What degrees, coursework, and other training have you had?

I have a bachelor's degree in psychology with a minor in music (of all things!). I was originally a music major, then a biology major, and finally a psychology major. I began psychology with an interest in research and experimental psych. and ended with a desire to work with children. I explored music therapy and working with developmentally disabled people before landing in probation.

Since graduation from college, I have attended numerous seminars and in-service training sessions on topics such as substance abuse; sexual offender dynamics and treatment; reality therapy [a counseling method that teaches people how to direct their lives]; transactional analysis [the parent–child–adult model of human interactions]; professional liability; the theories of Stanton Samenow; forensic diagnostics; children's code [law] updates; mid-life crisis; and the relationship between criminal behavior, bulimia, and anorexia. Because probation deals with such a wide variety of people who have such diverse problems, it is important to know as much about as many areas of dysfunction as possible. I also had some basic business courses such as typing and accounting. Believe it or not, they have come in very handy! Human services agencies never seem to have adequate clerical help, and I have had to type my own reports more than once.

What jobs have you held in human services?

I started right out of college in juvenile probation. I did internships while still in college, and I feel these are very valuable in helping a new graduate make a career choice. At the very least, internships let you decide what areas you definitely do not want to pursue. After 4 years as a juvenile probation officer, I moved to supervising adult offenders and took over coordination of the probation volunteer program. I became much more active and knowledgeable in volunteer management in the next 2 years. Most areas of human services are more than willing to allow employees to develop creative programs (volunteer programs are one example), as long as the employee is attending to his or her assigned duties.

Ten Years Later   I think it's much more difficult, for me anyway, to do the things that would be enjoyable to me. I became a supervisor in about 1993, and I supervised investigations, then I was moved to supervise specialized units. I have very little client contact anymore. That's frustrating because I'm so caught up with what I have to do to keep my job and my department moving on a day-to-day basis.

What are your likes and dislikes about working in human services? How have these changed over the years, if at all?

I came to the human services field as a probation officer, armed with theories, college-formed opinions, and principles and ideas of how the judicial system was going to function. I enjoyed working with "difficult" cases and spent many hours coordinating treatment plans and services for juvenile legal offenders. I was convinced that I wanted to work with juveniles until I died.

In college, there was a definite division between the behaviorists, the researchers, and the Freudians. I had chosen to identify with the Freudians. I believed very strongly in the Freudian principles and viewpoints, and I dealt with clients accordingly.

When I was a new probation officer, I saw human services as pretty clear cut, black and white. In those days, the solutions were clearer, the sources and causes of the problems were clearer, and the course of action to be pursued was clearest of all. Unfortunately, "the system" wouldn't always cooperate, nor would the clients! A dose of reality was so disheartening to this naive college graduate!

I no longer enjoy spending hours with an uncooperative client. I still enjoy working on difficult cases, but I no longer "waste" time on lengthy treatment plans with unwilling, resistive clients who deny any problems or responsibility for any problems.

There are certain options available in each situation. These options tend to overlap and/or have gaps in them. There is not always an applicable program available for a specific problem. Once the options are known, the client has certain choices.

It was startling to realize that not all people shared my value system! For example, while I may feel it is wrong for him or her to do so, a client may feel he or she has the right to continue breaking the law, to continue drinking alcohol to excess, or to continue using heroin. My job is to try to ensure that others are not hurt by a client's choice and that the client experiences the full impact of the consequences related to his or her choice. *I learned not to care more about the outcome of a situation than the client cares.* Needless to say, at this point, some behaviorist philosophy was creeping into my chosen Freudian approaches.

Effective human services workers are knowledgeable in many areas. They are able to assess and define problems and are then able to choose, from the vast reservoir of theories, treatment modalities, and service agencies, the treatment that best meets the client's needs. This sounds so simple, but it is not. Theories change, as do agencies and available services. Appropriate referrals necessitate ongoing monitoring and training.

An unfortunate reality of human services work is that most human services agencies receive government funding at some level. Working in a bureaucracy where program funding, salaries—and even some agency policies—are determined by legislative allocations is often frustrating. Individual employee incentives are few, and salaries are most often determined by a set classification system rather than by amount or quality of work. I have watched co-workers and friends in other human services agencies leave their jobs, and even the human services field, due to their frustrations with the effects of bureaucratic politics on their agency policies and funding and on their ability to work effectively with clients.

Human services jobs do not always fit the teachings of our youth: that if you work hard and do a good, conscientious job, good things will come to you. On the contrary, it is often the case that the harder you work, the higher the expectations of you become, but you will be paid the same as the guy next to you who does only what is required at a bare minimum!

What do you want to accomplish through your work? What rewards do you wish to receive? What has changed, if anything?

No longer do I wish to change the world. My goals have become more realistic and focused in relation to the confines and realities of the system in which I work. My rewards and satisfaction come from smaller-scale accomplishments, such as getting one client plugged into a complete program of services that enables him or her to feel happier and more comfortable with the world. Similarly, I feel satisfaction when a client feels more in control of his or her life and future path.

I plan more carefully for goals to be reached in the years to come and have learned to slow my pace in accordance with the snail-like pace of the governmental offices and agencies under whose guidelines I must operate. When I now look back, I can see my first 4 years as an orientation to the system in which I now operate. The next 4½ years show a steady, but slow, improvement in services and lines of communication. This is due in part to my work and level of understanding regarding the realities of "the system."

I want to prevent people from becoming heavily involved in crime by showing them effective alternatives to their present and/or past coping techniques. I want to feel that I am at least partly responsible for keeping the system accountable (the criminal justice system and related agencies). If nothing else, I want clients to see and experience the consequences of their actions so that they may make informed choices.

In some cases, I want the clients to know that there is someone who cares and will be honest and consistent in dealings with them.

I also work with community volunteers within the judicial system. I hope to see an accountable network of volunteer services recognized by the judicial system before I retire (or die). Working with judicial volunteers has been very rewarding. These people have become a support system for me, as they help to accomplish small goals to improve services within the judicial system. As our volunteer program has slowly expanded, it has become a political force that provides a powerful voice to elected officials.

Once a human services worker can identify "similar souls" in the community (and they are always there), these people can be organized into a very valuable support system and a very effective force for advocating needed changes. This type of support must be organized slowly and with foresight, to prevent formation of a radical and detrimental group.

In human services, workers sometimes feel isolated and alone. We forget that there are others (though not necessarily in a specific human services field) who share our views and ideals. These people may not have actual hours to contribute to improving the system, but they may be able to donate money or the political drive necessary to bring about desirable changes.

It has also become critical to me to see a more holistic view. In human services work, one can tend to focus only on one's clientele and their problems. One forgets the larger picture and may lose contact with the healthier part of society. This can give a rather morbid and depressed view of the world. *It is important to balance human services work with other interests that bring healthier contacts with other individuals whose problems are not your primary concern.*

For instance, it was so enlightening for me to speak at a local high school about the juvenile justice system. I saw kids who were actually planning to attend college! After 4 years of working with juvenile delinquents, my view had become skewed. I thought no young people were finishing high school, let alone considering college! This was a prime example of my human services work getting out of proportion and becoming too much of a priority!

Ten Years Later   I think a major change for me was the introduction of the cognitive restructuring approaches. The frustration I saw over the years in working with people on probation was that we could make some great changes and many of the offenders did very well when they were sitting with you, but when they went back to their environments, they didn't quite know how to implement what they had learned. We saw a lot of people that were fairly concrete in their thought process and to expect them to take what I talked about in one environment and abstract it into another, I think, was expecting far too much. My thought was if we could address cognitive process, then we might have an effect.

So at that time, the state brought in Dr. Robert Ross' program out of Canada, which had group sessions put together and used some of Goldstein's work on teaching social skills, critical reasoning, and management of emotions. It was just a wonderful program, and it had been validated in Canada on a couple of populations. It came into Colorado—we were the first state to start. I had wanted something like that, and I thought it was very valuable. I still think it is.

However, the state didn't do a real good job of picking facilitators; they kind of let anybody do it who wanted to. Also, a general problem with the state is that they implement programs, get them through the legislature, they bring in money for them, and then they dump them. The programs don't interrelate with one another, so we end up with duplication of services and major gaps in the system. Sometimes what appears logical, once studied, turns out to be ineffective and even detrimental. Programs should be empirically studied before widespread implementation.

So, I guess how things have changed for me is the answers are not as clear. When you come out of college the answers are clear because you've been taught how it should work, and you don't know that it won't, or you don't know that there is more to implementing something than just knowing the answers. I still think there are answers there, but as you gain more experience in the field you start to see that there's a lot more that influences the outcome than simply knowing the answer. It's important to understand the process necessary to achieve the "answer." You may need to alter your approach for offenders because of *their* cognitive process. There are many paths to the same destination—and a good human services worker should know as many of those paths as possible and continue to search for new ones—if they hope to be a resource for a person.

You can look at an individual and know what they need, but here come the other factors. Number one is the individual you're working with is not going to allow you in, is not going to follow your advice. You don't have the time that you should have. You don't have the resources that you should have. You feel they need some other services that you can't give them. Medical care, for example, particularly for the kinds of people I work with, is not available! I could get $1,000 for a psychological evaluation, but I couldn't get $250 for a physical to get a $35 pap smear for older female offenders who were either premenopausal or really pushing into menopausal years.

I think I'm a lot more open to what other people have to say. I don't think I'm as quick to rush in and say here's what I think we should do and how we should do it. I did mention, in my first interview, some of the politics that go on. I still work for the state. There are people I used to see when I was young and I'd say, "Gosh they're burned out, why don't they get out of the field?" I see now where that came from, that constant frustration. I think I'm still the creative person that I was 10 years ago. I still have ideas that I had 10 years ago, but I don't have as much time to implement them. In my last interview I said if you work for a state agency, they'll let you implement creative programs if you want to. They will, but only after they've exacted their pound of flesh for the week and you've done tons of work they put in front of you. You do all of this first, and then if you have time and the energy left and want to ignore your family, you can implement in *your* spare time.

There is a whole new era of probation officers coming up. I feel like I don't get the time to sit down with those new officers and toss out those little things that can really open their world, such as "Yeah, this is why the parents are looking at you funny, it's because you're 25 and they're 45, and you're trying to tell them they need parenting classes. Maybe that isn't something they want to hear." I remember when I first started as a supervisor, one of the young women under me was right out of college and in her 20s. Every case that came across my desk for a juvenile offender, she recommended the parents take parenting classes. I asked, "Why are you recommending this for every kid's parents?" and she goes, "Well the kid wouldn't be here if the parents were any good." Whoa! What a value statement. I had to stop that one. I said, "You know we need to take a critical look—there's some very, very good parents who have very troubled children. Many people and things can have an impact on a child, not *just* the parents. You need to look at why you're requiring that."

I think your perspective changes. I find myself these days thinking more along a continuum. Things don't upset me as much. It's like this is all just a big piece of the whole, it's not so much about win and lose or fail or success right now, it's more about "Where do we move on this continuum, which way did we move?" I think that's a big difference from where I was 10 years ago. Back then it was win or lose, a success or failure, that's where it had to be. I'm very definitely now where a couple of steps look as good.

When offenders come back to see me, surely I want to know if they've gotten into any more trouble, but what I think I want to hear them say is "you cared about me." That's become very important to me 'cause I want them to know that I did. There were people and there are people I've worked with that I don't like, but there are co-workers

I don't like either. I can still work with them and respect them as people. I think with legal offenders, even the very worst ones I saw, I was thinking, "How did this person get to this point? How did we not know this as a society? Is there another one somewhere going through this?"

Have you found it difficult to balance your personal and professional lives? If so, what works for you?

As a new probation officer, I used to spend many extra hours on client problems. I now believe clients must be given the opportunity to solve their own problems, and not having immediate access to me at all hours helps them to improve their own coping abilities. I am now able to tell a client who reaches me at night to call me in the morning, at work. Most problems can be dealt with the following day without a drastic change in the outcome. It also forces clients to plan ahead because they know you are only available to them at specific times.

I have come to realize that many of my clients expect me to be available to them at all times. However, they do not reciprocate the courtesy. If a client wants my services, it will need to be under my terms, which are *very* reasonable! There are always those clients for whom I will go the extra mile, but there are *many* who if given an inch will take a mile!

Balancing my personal and professional life has been difficult, especially since the birth of my first child in 1986. My son really forced me to reevaluate and change my priorities. Having a healthy balance in one's life, just like a balanced diet, is essential to one's emotional and physical well-being, as well as being essential to survival in a human services field.

Specifically, I no longer work extra hours. I pay close attention to quitting time and try to leave my work problems at the office. There is always tomorrow. I am fortunate to have a husband who was willing to give up his paid work to stay home with our son. So, the worry of day care has not been a problem for me. After working hours is my time for myself and my family. I try to give my family and myself the same quality of attention that I give to my clients during working hours.

Ten Years Later When you come out of high school and you make decisions in college and move out into the job market, you don't have life experience, nor do you have a lot of responsibility. Your personal life is very different so you can afford to focus everything on your career, and you have aspirations of where it's going to be. It doesn't occur to you that you're going to get older. It doesn't occur to you that you're going to not have the energy you had at 24. It doesn't occur to you that you're not going to want to work at home at night, that there are going be other interests in your life, like children. I have two children now, so that made a big difference. The direction that I'm taking and the rewards that I get, I'm a lot more involved with my family and the kids. They're real important to me, so I spend a lot of time with them doing what they need me to do, and they're not too impressed with my job.

Is there anything else you want to convey to people who are just starting out or who are already in human services?

I always advise new professionals to look carefully at the salary schedule for raises and decide whether to stay before they get too well-paid and can't afford to leave. What you need to do is pick a stopping point right before a scheduled big raise, and ask yourself, "Is this the organization, people, and work I want?" Also, remember people will not always reward you for doing a good job, so you need to have your own ideals and principles to sustain you.

Ten Years Later   I did a training workshop where I made the comment that I really didn't believe you could be as effective in working with offenders or people in general if you didn't care about them. I said, "You don't have to like what they do. You're gonna have a lot of issues with them, but you have to have a respect for them and a like for them as people. They're more likely to make changes for you if they feel respect and caring. Otherwise they're not going to pay any attention to what you say." A woman stood up and said she took exception to that, she said, "I don't like these people. I think they've done horrible things, and I think some of them are scum. I don't think that affects my ability to ensure that the orders of the court are carried out." There was no point in arguing with the woman. She is totally ineffective. No offender is going to listen to her.

I'm starting to think there are some people who go into human services because of their personality style, a nurturing personality. It's not that you choose human services necessarily and then perceive those things that make you a good human services worker. Having trained a lot of probation officers, I really believe that there are certain ones that come in, and the skill is there, because they are nurturing people, caring individuals. The hard part is to get them to draw the line as to how far they can go with a client. No, you don't invite the person over to your home for dinner, you can't give them money, you can't store their things for them. You have to draw that line, "I care, I'll cry for you, I feel bad for what's happened to you. Here's what we gotta do, and I'm gonna help you do it. But yes, if you tell me you committed a crime, I'm going to report it." I used to tell new offenders, "It's like your mother. You go to prison, your mother will always go to the prison to visit you, but she can't break you out. She'll share all your sorrows, she'll still love you, but you're still in prison, and she knows that. It doesn't diminish her love or her caring for you, but there's only so much a caring person can do or accept responsibility for."

I think we don't look hard enough in the field to find that nurturing personality and hire it. What sounds good on paper doesn't necessarily translate into the ability to *effectively* empathize or to convey caring within the confines of the job, to the offender. I think to some extent we can teach someone who does not have that personality to manage people, but oh my gosh, what we lose in those positions and what we could have. I'm not referring to what the cops always call "bleeding heart liberals." No, no, no. These are realistic individuals who care about the people around them. It's so interesting how in one venue you get an award, and people say you're a loving, caring individual—the police give the same awards as we do—but on the other hand you're a bleeding heart liberal. Well, there can be a middle ground. I've had offenders that have said to me, "Cheryl is really a witch; she's the worst person I've ever met." I used to tell new probation officers, "As a supervisor that's how I know you're doing a good job: if half your caseload hates you and half of them love you." If everyone totally adores their worker, then I wonder who's manipulating whom.

Helping people make changes, real changes, is hard, and people don't make changes if they're comfortable. Sometimes we are the catalyst for creating discomfort or dissonance, which makes change necessary and desirable. Workers must be secure enough with themselves that they're not looking to the client for self-affirmation. Yet, they must be open to criticism from the client, to facilitate their own growth as a human services worker. It's a difficult balance. Human services workers must constantly evaluate themselves, their approach, their style, their objectivity, their skills, their knowledge base, but they must also be able to make decisions for the client, based on facts and critical reasoning—even when the decision is difficult and the client is condemning the worker!

Human services workers must also be able to acknowledge mistakes. We make them—it's a part of our learning and growth—and offenders can then see us as human. But I definitely see a difference between making a decision based on respect and care for the client that later turns out to be in error, and making a decision based on personal needs, or our own agenda, without care and respect for the client. A mistake based in care and respect leads to learning. *Always listen to and consider the client's point of view no matter how distasteful. It is only by hearing them and trying to understand that we can expect to be heard, heard and understood.* If you hear and try to understand, you can learn and grow, and that's a big part of what I'm here for!

Exercise

9-1. Consider these questions:
    a. Which aspect of this interview do you identify with?
    b. How has Cheryl changed during her career?
    c. What lessons do you find in Cheryl's interview that you think are important for human services professionals?

PROFILE: MARY ANNE HARVEY

Mary Anne Harvey was 39 and Executive Director of The Legal Center, a protection and advocacy organization for people with disabilities, when the author interviewed her for the first edition. Ten years later Mary Anne is still Executive Director of The Legal Center. Here is what she had to say then and now.

What degrees and other training do you have?

I have a bachelor's degree in English. I was a literature student. When I finished my undergraduate degree, I started a master's program in English at Wichita State University, and the first year of that program I got my teaching credentials. My goal in life at that point was to be an English teacher, and I did that for about 6 months. I substitute taught in the public schools in Gillette, Wyoming.

What jobs have you held in human services?

My former husband came home from work one day and said the local day care center needed a director. I knew nothing about preschool children, although I knew lots about adolescent development. I did know something about business. I had the secretarial and bookkeeping skills I had obtained to support myself through school. So I applied for the job and was hired.

So at age 24, I became the director of a county child care agency that served preschool children, most of whom were 3–5 years old. About 25% of the children had special needs of some kind, from [children] needing a couple hours a week of speech therapy or language development to children who were very severely multiply disabled. These children were fully integrated into our program; at the time, I didn't know that there was any other way to do preschool.

The first year I spent playing catch-up in terms of my own knowledge about early childhood development and what was available. I had a sense from what I knew about how kids learn and the kind of setting I wanted to work in that I didn't like the way the preschool was structured. So I gathered up all of my teachers one day and drove over to see a Montessori preschool. I just said, "Let's go observe for a day," and lo and behold, as we were driving back everybody said, "Gosh, we could do some of that stuff." Then we started doing a lot of reading and in-service training about individual programming for preschool kids and how one sets up such programs. We called on a couple of very good resources. For instance, there was a professor at the University of Wyoming who did several in-service training sessions with us. And a number of us were involved in starting an early childhood association, so I got training there. Also, in the summer of 1975, I talked my board into sending me to a 3-week day care management seminar. I had some very intensive day care management training at that point. So, yes, there was a lot of training along the way, but other than the day care management experience, I had no administrative training.

During that time, I had gotten very interested in family counseling. I had received a lot of in-service training in early childhood education, behavior modification, and in family counseling and dynamics and how they affect a child's life. My ex-husband and I did some co-therapy with the families at the day care center that worked out very nicely. As a result of this, I applied to a couple of graduate schools to get a master's in social work with an emphasis in family counseling. I had been accepted at the University of Kansas when I was contacted by the deputy director of Rocky Mountain Planned Parenthood in Denver. (I had been involved in starting a Planned Parenthood clinic in Gillette.) The director of development was leaving [his position] and said, "You really ought to think about this job."

That was when I decided I would probably stay in human services administration. My observation at that point was that some human services agencies were managed badly and had many problems and that people did not bring good business practices and principles to the human services field. I thought that was outrageous. Bad management caused a tremendous waste of money and people's time and was unfair to the people who didn't get good services. So, I decided if I was going to stay in human services, I would end up in administration. I was convinced I could do it better than anybody else, which sounds sort of egotistical I guess, but my administrative skills are strong, and it is something I enjoy.

I also decided at that point that if I was going to do that, I really had to have fund-raising skills. So, for 3 years at Planned Parenthood I did fund-raising. They had been willing to hire me with no fund-raising skills. That was a really good experience, plus I learned a lot from Sheri Tepper, the Executive Director at Planned Parenthood. She was a bright, innovative person and a very strong manager. We didn't always agree, but even now sometimes I'll do certain things, and if I stop and think about it, I know I learned that from Sheri Tepper. The older I get, the more I understand decisions she made at the time that I didn't agree with then, which I probably would agree with now. Plus, Planned Parenthood at that time attracted a collection of other people who had started out in a lot of other fields. We had people in business administration, we had a former nun who had been an English teacher, we had people who were in nursing and were going into administration. So I worked with this group of very bright people who were about my age, who had come from diverse backgrounds, and who were interested in family-planning services for poor people.

Then, I answered an ad that said The Legal Center needed an executive director. That summer, 1980, I had been taking a class from Denver Free University called "Which Job is Me?" The first exercise we did in the class was to write a classified advertisement for the job that we really wanted. And, except for the fact that the ad I wrote was for a child care center, and there was a little difference in salary because we were supposed to write our ideal ad, the ad that appeared for The Legal Center position was almost word for word what I had written in class. It was unreal. It was one of those things that you look at and say, "I don't believe this!" It was the only time I had ever gotten a job for which I felt I had the skills, where someone said this is what we want you to do, and I said I can do all of those things. Up until then I had done stuff I wasn't trained to do (except for teaching).

The Legal Center serves people with disabilities who have legal problems in which the disability is central to the problem. This includes everything from employment discrimination, to Social Security eligibility, to obtaining legally mandated services. When I first started with The Legal Center, it was already the designated protection and advocacy system in Colorado for people with developmental disabilities. It has since become the designated protection and advocacy system for people with mental illnesses and the designated client assistance program for people served by our state vocational rehabilitation system.

What are your likes and dislikes about working in human services? How have these changed over the years, if at all?

I think what has always attracted me, and probably is also the reason I tried to become a teacher, was that I really felt this kind of work makes a difference in people's lives. Day care is very important to parents, and it's important that children have every edge they can possibly get before they get into school. To be involved in that, plus offer children an opportunity to go to school with other children who are different from them was a real plus. I didn't realize until 1975 how innovative Wyoming was in terms of its preschool services. There were 17 day-training centers for preschoolers across the state. It was impressive to me that people identified a need and addressed it and did so in a meaningful way in a state that is very sparsely populated. Certainly not every one of those 17 day-training centers was in a fully integrated setting, but they all had pacesetters. There was just sort of a spirit about it, plus I loved the people that I worked with. It was fun, hard work; I felt like I was accomplishing something. We would see children come into our program with 18- to 20-month delays in terms of where they should have been chronologically. We would see them catch up over a period of time and know that they would be okay. That's very satisfying.

The thing that drives me crazy and makes me want to run away is when people don't take this business seriously. I think that's one of the things that makes me really sick and angry about what's happened here recently. We've lost a major program in the community because of mismanagement and irresponsibility, and that damages every single one of the people who were being served by that agency as well as other disability programs and nonprofit organizations in the community. That's intolerable.

I came to The Legal Center from Planned Parenthood because I like being the executive director. I decided that I would rather be in this supervisory position than in a middle management position. I think people who are executive directors have a fair need for control. My protection and advocacy colleagues chuckle about that from time to time.

What has kept me at The Legal Center is a couple of things. One of them is the working relationship I have with Randy Chapman, the Director of Legal Services. We have been able to work it out so we don't get in each other's way. We really had to struggle with that a couple of times over the years. The other thing is just the nature of advocacy. The whole civil rights area becomes such a central part of your life. The problem is what do you do after you've been a protection and advocacy director? Where do you go from here? Well, maybe one of the reasons we're building our national association, one of the things we talk and dream about, is so that we will have a national training institute for advocates where people might have an opportunity to either go into another agency for a period of time or to an institute setting for a week and do some training and some teaching. We have a pool of incredible skill and knowledge across the country. The other thing that has kept us here, a lot of us, is the growth of the program. I think had the program been decimated, had we not had the opportunity for growth by adding the protection and advocacy system for the mentally ill and for the Client Assistance Program, a lot of us would have left because the challenge wouldn't have been as great.

The other thing that is so interesting about advocacy is that there are times when it is really very funny. The situations some people get into are outrageous. What I have noticed about very good advocates is that they have a marvelous sense of humor, and I think that is what helps us survive.

Ten Years Later   I still can't think of what else I would rather do, unless it would be not to work at all [laughter]. I have thought about this a lot for the last couple of years because I've been at The Legal Center 17 years now. I've been here so long that every 18 months or so I feel this need to revisit whether my time and effectiveness has passed and whether or not I need to move on. I've done a lot of examination about that, and I looked at other career possibilities and looked at other organizations and sometimes other businesses, but this organization is still developing and is still new. I still come to work wondering what's going to happen at The Legal Center today, and I still love working with Randy Chapman. It's been a wonderful collegial partnership that we've had, and I've been very fortunate to have that in my work. I've had an opportunity to influence change, to help our national association grow, to see a lot of positive changes in the laws for people with disabilities, and to feel like the organization has really had a significant impact. I just don't know where [else] I would have all of those things, plus a level of independence here that is really quite remarkable. And so when I think about what would I rather be doing, I would really probably be cooking and gardening and reading the newspaper every morning and reading my books and fluffing my nest.

Are there other things that have changed about why you do what you do? What's good about it for you? Have the rewards changed?

What I see about myself is that I have become a whole lot tougher. When I was going to Wichita State University, one of my favorite books was *Teaching as a Subversive Activity* [Postman & Weingartner, 1969]. The authors said that if you were going to be a good teacher you had to have a good "crap detector." I think that's important in whatever line of work you do, particularly in human services. People used to describe me as a very nice person, and I used to hate it. *You could go through your whole life as a nice person and not make a damned bit of difference.* I think I really like what I've learned as an advocate about being a tougher, stronger person and not allowing people to get away with things that I would have let them get away with before. Not that I think that we go about advocacy in an aggressive or adversarial way, but we have an assertive style that we use that is very consistent in terms of how we approach problems. Internally, I find that I am not patient with a lot of things that I used to worry about. I don't tolerate some bureaucratic hassles that I would have probably let go 5 or 6 years ago when I first started in this job. I push the system in terms of my working with the people in it because I don't think we need to be pushed around. So that's something that I can feel has changed. People who have known me over a period of time have commented on that.

In terms of what else is different, I've become more cynical. It was really good for us to have a couple of college interns around this past summer, people who have a very fresh and new perspective. It was fun to be in a relationship where I had an opportunity to do some teaching with them.

Ten Years Later   I've been thinking about how my own attitudes have changed about being a manager, because I guess what's happened in the last 10 years is that the organization continued pretty dramatically to grow up until this past year. In 1994 we received a very large grant from HUD [Housing and Urban Development], and we opened the Grand Junction office. We had some contractors leaving the organization at the time, but we also did not fill some vacancies because I was anticipating that we were going to transfer some funding if the HUD grant was not renewed, which in fact it was not. We'd gone through this tremendous growth and then a period where we laid off people, so there's been a lot of loss in the organization in the last couple of years.

You can read about theory and practice of management in terms of having to downsize and making the decision to do it, and what it does to an organization is just astounding to me. We have been recovering from the layoffs for a year and are just beginning to feel, I'm just beginning to feel now that the organization again is pretty much on an even keel. And four people who were very close to the organization, three of whom were employees and one who was a contractor, have passed away while they were working for us, so my perspective about what those kinds of very traumatic events [deaths and downsizing] do to an organization has really changed a lot.

To get us [through these traumas], I've probably more closely managed this organization in the last 2 years than I have certainly for the previous 5 or 6. I've had a lot more personal interaction with people at all levels of the organization, pretty much felt like we really had to deal with the anger, which was part of the fallout of the layoffs, people's jobs being threatened. People in the organization have told me that nobody felt as if their job was safe. I don't know that there was anything we could have done differently to make people feel more secure because, in fact, we looked across the board at what made the most sense for the organization for the future. I feel like I've been wrapping my arms around the organization, sort of trying to keep people together.

Have you found it difficult to balance your personal and professional lives? If so, what works for you?

It's very difficult based on the goals you set for yourself if you're a superachiever. I think that women are under a lot of pressure to do it all. In the last 3 years, I have been president of a nonprofit organization which filed under Chapter 11 bankruptcy to reorganize one of its corporations 2 years ago; I had to facilitate the board's making that decision and stay involved while they worked that out. And I've been president of the National Association of Protection and Advocacy Systems (NAPAS). There have been times when the stress was just so incredible I wondered what in the hell I was doing. What I learned from all of that is that there probably aren't very many crises that would throw me. It would have to be just a major catastrophic event that would really undo me.

When I left the presidency of the nonprofit organization, I was literally counting the minutes. At my last board meeting, I said, "My term will be over in 18 hours, 34 minutes, and 25 seconds." The bankruptcy proceedings were the worst experience of my life. I had people yelling at me, and it was awful. I could not have done that without the support of The Legal Center board, because I was spending a lot of hours on that. Certainly, when I took that presidency I had no idea what was going to happen.

Brad (my current husband) has been enormously supportive. We've just sort of had to work through it as it's happened and really go out of our way to plan time together. His schedule is every bit as busy as mine is. This year, I decided that I was only going to do those things that I consider fun and that my reward for going through all of this for the last 3 years is that I'm only going to do things that will not add a significant amount of stress to my life. I'm no longer president of NAPAS—I did love that experience—and I'm going off the other board since I've been there for 8 or 9 years, and I'm starting school. I'm starting school not because I need the degree, but because I really would like to have the theory catch up with the practice. I like to learn, and when I was being recruited to enroll for this program, the administrator said that I should take at least two classes a semester or I'd never finish. I don't have to do that. If I want to take 6 years to finish this program, the catalog says I can do it. And if I only want to take one class a semester, there is nothing that precludes my doing it. I'm trying to get rid of night meetings. So I think Brad and I are both trying to figure out ways that we can spend a little more time together and have more time at home. It requires a concerted effort.

If you choose to, you can allow yourself to work all the time, and it's not healthy. I think those long, long hours and the high stress over time are why people leave the field, because they can't take it. You've got to build in some fun so you keep your perspective healthy, so you can continue to do the work that you want to. You really have to find that balance. I certainly would not want to trade my marriage for my work.

Ten Years Later   Last year I was chairing our national organization's committee on the development of outcomes. Even though that was another piece of work, it took me out of town, and it was done with my colleagues, so it was really an opportunity to be with them and to be supported by them. I took the time to visit several very dear friends, one in Atlanta, one in Racine, Wisconsin. So, there were things I did very specifically to sort of attend to my own needs, but it's been a really incredible year.

On the personal front there's been lots of responsibility. Brad's disabled brother is living with us. My mother has had two surgeries in the last 18 months, and my parents have moved out of the house they have lived in for, I don't know, 14 or 15 years. They just finished that move this month. Plus through part of the time in the last 5 years Brad's son has been with us. He is grown, and that was a great pleasure to have him in our lives because for 15 years when he was growing up with his mother in Montana, there was no contact between Brad and him. So, to have him reconnect with his dad and to give us both the opportunity to get to know him was really wonderful. I think I have to give Brad a lot of credit for really being very supportive and waking up with a smile on his face in the morning and being the happy little guy he generally is, because that's helped a lot. Our marriage has been good, and I've been really grateful for that, because it would have been very hard, I think, to do this work if my close personal life was also in crisis.

One of the things I said to myself is that I really want to have more fun this year, so we're working on that both at home and here. I can see the staff starting to relax a little bit here and starting to get excited again about some of the things that are on the horizon and people sort of dropping by and chatting with me a little more than they did 6 months ago or so, which says I'm more available and they are too. So that's fun. We've got some people who are new to the organization and very excited about being here. That's always fun. They're very excited about everything—the staff in Grand Junction is remarkable in that perspective. They really are very enthusiastic and very supportive of the organization.

Is there anything else you want to convey to people who are just starting out or who are already in human services?

I would say to try to seek the balance between your work and your personal life as early as you can, because it's a good habit to get into. I think in the long run it will strengthen rather than weaken your professional opportunities.

Ask a lot of questions. Find out about the organizations you work for, how they're managed, how they're run; and understand their history. That's one of the things I've really come to understand as being very important. I don't think we as human services directors teach that enough, nor do I think people go out of their way to seek it out. How people will fit into an organization at any given time has a lot to do with the history of the organization. You can learn a lot by just taking a look at that and hearing stories of the organization. There are formal and informal histories of an organization that are important, vital, and instructive.

Learn to congratulate yourself when you've accomplished something because in this work you may not be congratulated by others. Sometimes, you have to be satisfied with just knowing you've done a good job.

For managers, it's important to let your staff know they're part of a team and to acknowledge their achievements publicly.

Ten Years Later   I think it's probably harder in human services right now. I was reading through this book [the first edition] last night and I don't know that the prospects for being wealthy are any better now than they were when the book first came out. I think that managed care has changed a lot of things. We at The Legal Center are exploring what our role in managed care is going to be and [what our role] in dispute resolution in managed care [will be] in every system that we deal with. I think that this work still provides a really wonderful alternative to traditional business, and I find lawyers very much wanting to work in the public interest arena after having worked in a law firm where the practice of law was very different and they didn't feel like they were representing the good guys. I don't think we're going to see anymore big right-to-treatment lawsuits, and partly because those lawsuits were successful in achieving what a lot of them set out to do. Some of them are still ongoing with monitors, and they've taken tremendous resources, so I think we take a different look at how we use resources. I see that happening throughout the nonprofit sector. I went to a conference this week, and there was a lot of discussion about sustainability, how we build our communities. [We discussed] how we deal with differences among factions of people, factions of nonprofit organizations, belief systems that are constantly at loggerheads with one another, and what that means for those of us who really want to support the concept of community and inclusion. So, those are still very much issues, and the focus has shifted a little bit, I think. *But it's still very much the role of the human services sector and the nonprofit arena to be an underpinning in the community for values, for hope for people.*

It's still a great field, and I would recommend for people to certainly explore opportunities if that's something that they want to do. I think that there may also be more opportunities for entrepreneurial work in the human services sector than there have been before. I think that people are looking at ways organizations can make money to sustain themselves in the future, so that raises some opportunities for people who enjoy that kind of thing.

Exercise

9-2.   Again, consider the questions:
    a.   Can you identify with any aspect of this interview?
    b.   How has Mary Anne changed during her career?
    c.   What lessons do you find in Mary Anne's interview that you think are important for human services professionals?

Ellen Berlin

Whatever the field is, I just think sometimes we get so centered in our work and our philosophy that we forget to see all people as individuals with their own strengths and with their own weaknesses, just like I have my own strengths and my own weaknesses. We need somehow to value all our lives, just be able to really hear each other and somehow go from there. I guess I would encourage us all and people going into it to try to take a look at their misconceptions before they walk in the door.

Suzanne Cardiff

Keep life simple. I tell myself that every day. Sometimes you get so caught up in cases of people. There's so many things they teach you in training like "Don't work harder than your client 'cause then you know it's not doing any good." So, you have to keep yourself in check. It's what I do with myself a lot. I think, "Am I judging this person too much, am I putting too much pressure on this person?" You gotta think, "Well what if I was this person. . . ." I think that's the biggest thing: You gotta put yourself in their shoes, you gotta think, "If I was this person and somebody came in and told me 'Do this and this and this and this and this,' how would I react?" So, you gotta think "What approach would work on me if I was in their situation?" You don't have to have been abused or have grown up in a poverty-stricken home to know.

Heidi Daly

I would suggest not limiting yourself to one aspect of the work, to one direction in human services. Broaden the view of your experiences so you have your choice of what to go into. Then if you realize that it's not for you at some point in time, you have another direction to go into without getting out of human services. My one regret is that I'm not directly in human services right now; I would like to be sometime soon. I don't think I can go back in the nursing homes because of the way things are, and I don't have experience in other areas, so it'll be difficult for me to get back into it. Someday I will.

Jennifer Echarte

I don't know what to say to people who are burnt out, people who just are going through the motions but have shut off completely their emotional contact. You know how after a while of working with your hands, you build calluses? That's what these people have got going. I have that a little bit. There are times when I get choked up, and I cry, and I feel so bad for a boy. I hope I don't lose that. I don't know how to tell somebody to continue to feel no matter how much it costs.

I remember in my psychology classes in college, there were some people in the class that believed that they had never had any problems in their lives—they had a great upbringing and a great life, and everything's great. They have to learn somehow to relate to somebody who has only known problems. There's a certain amount of open-mindedness that you have to have to relate to people. There's a piece of it that is about not judging other people. There's times where a kid I work with will run away, get drunk, and steal a car and trash it, and I won't say that's acceptable, but I don't come down so hard I've taken the relationship away either. I don't say, I worked so hard with this kid, and look at what he did.

I'm 24 years old, and I still have a lot of hope in me and a lot of excitement about life. That's what I bring to my clients. I just hope that somebody would know you have to be firm, and you have to be not pushed around by the population because with the adolescents, with adults, everybody knows the system. I've seen so much of human nature, and human nature is sort of a study for me. I like to explore it and understand that every client is a new way for me to understand what people are like.

There are some people that are so caught up in having everything controlled and being nice and neat and organized—and in this field, nothing is going to be nice and neat and organized. It's not your place to say you don't think that their ideas are right. You have to be able to let people explore things for themselves and learn lessons for themselves. Flexibility is what I would hope people could have going in.

William Esp

What I wish I'd known earlier, with all this knowledge and experience and gaining wisdom, is that you move away [from those who have been in your life] unless people are going with you [changing in similar ways]. Even explaining your changes is difficult because it may sound condescending or that you're putting yourself above them. It's not that they're not smart enough or that I'm better, but a lot of times even trying to explain that to them, it comes off as that and it's very painful. That might have been something I wish I would have known. I don't know how it would have affected me, but I just think it's something good to know in terms of preparing yourself to do this.

The only other thing I wish I'd known earlier is where the field was going politically. It is really scary, and we need people in this field and good people more than ever, but things overall don't seem to be getting better. They just seem to be getting crazier. However, a question I always have is are things really getting crazier, or is it just as I do my own work I become more sensitive? My guess is that it's probably a combination of both.

What keeps me here, a lot of it was and still is about healing myself. Sometimes I think I hear therapists or counselors, whoever, say you can't do that, you're here for the patient. I can't imagine anyone getting into this work that didn't sort of at least to some degree have that drive [to heal] going for them. I think it's just so important to acknowledge that so you can work with [personal issues] consciously. If you don't acknowledge it, then you deal unconsciously, and you can't make conscious choices about how you work with it in your work with others.

Pamela Meister

I saw myself as a liberal, a very strong liberal [before working as a patient representative], but I have seen patients here who are part of the system who don't need to be part of the system. So, before I probably would have said everyone who was on that program needed to be on there, [but] what I've learned is that there are people who do really scam the system or do feel that they are owed. That was a real eye opener for me.

I think your heart has to be there. I think that has to be your value, if you want to be in any area where helping others is your priority. If you're in it for financial gain, that won't happen. But for me feeling good about what I do was really more important than the paycheck.

Christa Pavlus

I think that finding that balance and keeping your personal life healthy is very, very important in order to do a good job when you're at work. Because if you come in feeling, "Oh my God, it's another day," then that's how your whole day is going to go. And if you come in feeling upbeat, even if your job is dealing with death or dealing with illness or unhappiness for people, you have to look at it in a different way. You can't always look at death as negative, as unhappiness for people because it is not always negative. You have to find a different way of looking at things. That's a very important part of learning to give in human services, that there is a different way to look at everything. You have to find humor in things, appropriately. You have to look for the positives instead of focusing on the negatives—there tend to be a lot of them in this setting (but I don't see them as negatives any more). When you first come in you think, "Nursing home or long-term care, oh my god, that's a place to come and die," and I really consider it a place to come and live. I think we just have to change our focus a lot. The biggest thing to remember is don't come in with a closed mind because if you leave your options open, you will find a lot of positives and a lot of joy and a lot of pleasure in it.

Cathy Phelps

I believe that I've been really sort of blessed and fortunate to do a lot of things and be sort of personally and professionally challenged. I've been able to sort of integrate those things in my personal relationships in a positive way. I think initially when I started out it wasn't [like] that. It was more self-righteousness and dogmatic and platformish, more "you have to do it this way, sister, you have to do it this way." Now I feel like

I can still have an impact, make statements, and be who I am and not be apologetic for it. I didn't have to adopt a costume— I can be comfortable in many places. There are places that I'm not comfortable, and recognizing that there are things I don't want to do was a good thing. There are people that I don't want to extend myself to, and that was okay too. I'm talking about colleagues and about boards that I don't want to sit on. So, that feels really good, being able to set limits. Particularly being an African American, in the past I felt when people asked me, I had to do it, I had to be representative, there had to be a voice there. Now I let people find their own way.

Ten years ago, fifteen years ago, I would have said "Oh, you know, it's been so rewarding, I want to help people," that kind of thing, and someone said to me, "Cathy, if you want to help people, get a job at a gas station. That is not what this is about, that is not what you should be thinking. It's not that self-sacrificing." I think there was also some "glamour" associated with it, "Oh you do that, that must be so rewarding. You must be such a good person, I couldn't do that"—so I think that was also part of it.

I realized whatever little piece I was carving out, the difference I was making or helping to start, that was good enough for me. That was where my heart was, working on issues that intertwine ethnicity and gender and violence and health and being able to use lots of tools to make a difference. I didn't have to use the standard support group manual if I wanted to bring in literature or videos or go to a restaurant or take a library tour. I can create therapeutic change by using different kinds of tools and strategies, so I think that's how I've changed.

To people just starting their careers, I would say be prepared to work hard, be adventurous. One of the things that I encourage my students to do is to stretch, to step outside of academia, the environment that they grew up in, and have a different kind of experience, sort of a Peace Corps experience, somewhere with someone, not so much to see how they can help but what did they learn about themselves, about their story. Service learning is what we call it at the community college where I teach. I think that really can help you do your best work. It's not about always helping people pick up their legs and feet and helping them walk, it's trying to figure out the long sweep of your own history, your own story, and what that may mean to somebody else, and what their story will mean to you. The only way you get those kinds of experiences is to stretch, to step outside and do something that you wouldn't ordinarily be comfortable doing or be interested in doing. I think that really makes a difference when you're working with people.

Johnn Young

You definitely can be emotionally rich, you can get definitely all your needs met, and your creature comforts met, but I don't see me getting filthy rich financially from this, that's what I wish I had known.

If you'd asked anyone, from when I started doing this work, probably 5 or 6 years ago, they would say, "Well, he's blossomed, he's slowly coming into his own."

What I would like to say to other people starting out is that it's rewarding for me. I have to evaluate on an ongoing daily basis what I'm doing, why I'm doing it, and if I want to keep doing it. If it turns out that I don't want to keep doing it, I need to be the first one to know, not have somebody come in and say it looks like it's stressed you out here, maybe you need to do something else. I evaluate myself on an ongoing daily basis because if I don't like what I'm doing, I shouldn't be doing it, and because if I don't like what I'm doing, I'm not of service to anybody.

Have my answers to these questions changed over time? No, they've not. That's a good thing because it means that the answers are solid, it means that they come from a solid base, it means that they're not in flux like everything else in the world.

Exercise

9-3.   Consider these questions:
   a.   Can you identify with any aspect of these interviews?
   b.   What lessons do you find in these interviews that you think are important for human services professionals?

REFLECTIONS ON THE INTERVIEWS

The human services professionals interviewed for this book have provided a wide range of thoughtful answers to the questions raised at the beginning of the book. Here, once more, are those questions:

Why did you choose to do human services work? What do you expect to get out of doing human services work? In other words, what are your rewards?

The people with whom the author spoke do human services work because they want to make a positive difference in people's lives and because they want to learn and grow and change. They value connections with people, both those whom they serve and their colleagues.

They are not starry-eyed: They are clear about the negative aspects of working in human services, particularly political and bureaucratic obstacles and low salaries. They struggle to provide effective services in the face of systemic obstacles and limited tangible rewards.

What do you expect to accomplish?

None of them expects to accomplish exactly the same thing, but all have a strong sense of what they want to accomplish. Most focus on changes in the lives of individuals; some focus on changes in systems or other professionals.

What are your values as you provide services?

The value most often expressed by the 11 interviewees is respect for the people they serve. Many also believe it is important to collaborate with clients rather than do things for them.

How should you act while you provide services?

One answer appears in every interview, namely the importance of continued growth, of always learning more about oneself and about how to be a more effective professional.

Another common theme is learning to speak up, to identify what is important about your work and set limits about what you can and cannot do.

How do you manage the stress of working in human services?

Everyone who was interviewed spoke about the importance of self-care and effective stress management. Many discussed their continued efforts to develop better skills in this area, and all agreed it is essential to balance the professional and personal parts of their lives.

A FINAL VISIT WITH DIANA

As she finishes reading the section above, Diana says to herself, "Do I wish I'd read these interviews *before* I got into human services! I guess what I've been doing with my support group is trying to find my answers to those questions.

"Wow. A year ago, I never thought I'd last beyond a week. It's been tough, real tough at times, but I stuck with it. I don't think I'll be a probation officer all my life, but it's okay right now. Maybe I'll talk to my supervisor next week about where to go from here.

"Oh, it's nearly time to meet the group for our first annual support celebration. Seems a far cry from a year ago."

CHOICES IN PROFESSIONAL DEVELOPMENT

> *What can I say? There comes a moment, as who knows*
> *better than you, when one has to move forward, when it is*
> *impossible to stay in the same place without moving back.*
> *(Cross, 1984, p. 19)*

People pursue career development for a variety of reasons. You may have a long-term goal that requires several developmental steps. You may be bored with your present job and wish to develop new skills. You may enjoy learning for its own sake. There is no one right way to develop your career in human services work. Here are some possibilities:

- Develop your clinical skills by enrolling in additional training programs.
- Become an administrator or manager of human services.
- Become a teacher of human services professionals.
- Change the types of people you serve (e.g., switch from work with children who have been abused to work with older adults).
- Move into policy design or quality assurance work at a state or federal agency.
- Become an advocate for systems change within the field of human services.
- Combine your expertise in human services with professional training in law, medicine, or business.
- Become a consultant to service providers.
- Engage in applied research in the human services.
- Write about human services work.

Consider that careers do not move in nice straight lines: neither does a person's professional growth. What interests or motivates you now is not necessarily what will interest or motivate you 5 years from now. That is why it is helpful to ask yourself the questions in the following exercise once a year. If your answers next year are different from the answers you give today, then that does not mean anything is wrong. It means that your professional goals have changed, so your plans need to change to match your goals.

Exercise

9-4.   What are your long-term professional goals?
    a.   Five years from now, what do you want your work life to be like?
    b.   What skills do you want to have that you do not have now?
    c.   What professional knowledge do you want to have that you do not have now?
    d.   What do you want your job title to be?
    e.   Where do you want to be working?
    f.   What do you want your annual salary to be?
    g.   What associations do you want to belong to?
    h.   What awards do you want to earn?
    i.   What balance do you want to have between your personal and professional lives?   (Scott, 1980)

A FINAL WORD

These are not easy times for professional helpers. The naive optimism of the 1960s, when my generation thought solutions to all the world's social ills were at hand, is long gone. Cuts in government funding for social services and education are routine, and private donations are increasingly hard to come by. Society is more ready to punish people who act out than it is to fund programs that prevent such problems in the first place. It would be easy to respond to current conditions with the pessimistic assumption that effective human services are no longer possible. I do not believe that to be the case.

I have spent more than 30 years working in human services, education, and health care. Writing the second edition of this book was a wonderful reminder of how much I like the people who are professional helpers. I am still, in Goodman's words that open this book, unimpressed "by the heroics of the people convinced they are about to change the world" (1979, p. 19). I am still "more awed by the heroism of those who are willing to struggle to make one small difference after another" (p. 20). This book is for the people who change the world by making one small difference after another.

REFERENCES

Academy releases report on boosting human performance. (1994). *APS Observer, 7*(5), 1, 14–19.

Anderson, R.A. (1978). *Stress power: How to turn tension into energy.* New York: Human Services Press.

Andresen, G. (1995). *Caring for people with Alzheimer's disease: A training manual for direct care providers.* Baltimore: Health Professions Press.

Auerbach, S.M., & Gramling, S.E. (1998). *Stress management: Psychological foundations.* Upper Saddle River, NJ: Prentice Hall.

Axtell, R.E. (1991). *Gestures: The do's and taboos of body language around the world.* New York: John Wiley & Sons.

Bateson, M.C. (1989). *Composing a life.* New York: Atlantic Monthly Press.

Bernstein, D.A., & Borkovec, T.D. (1973). *Progressive relaxation training: A manual for the helping professions.* Champaign, IL: Research Press.

Bernstein, G.S., Ziarnik, J.P., Rudrud, E.H., & Czajkowski, L.A. (1981). *Behavioral habilitation through proactive programming.* Baltimore: Paul H. Brookes Publishing Co.

Blanchard, K., Carlos, J.P., & Randolph, A. (1996). *Empowerment takes more than a minute.* San Francisco: Berrett-Koehler.

Bramson, R.M. (1981). *Coping with difficult people.* New York: Ballantine Books.

Bridges, W. (1998). *Surviving corporate transition: Rational management in a world of mergers, layoffs, start-ups, takeovers, divestitures, deregulation, and new technologies.* New York: Bantam Doubleday Dell.

Brody, J. (1990). *Jane Brody's good food book: Living the high carbohydrate way.* New York: Bantam Doubleday Dell.

Christensen, K., Haroun, A., Schneiderman, L.J., & Jeste, D.V. (1995). Decision-making capacity for informed consent in the older population. *Bulletin of the American Academy of Psychiatry & the Law, 23*(3), 353–365.

Covey, S. (1989). *The seven habits of highly effective people.* New York: Simon & Schuster.

Cowan, J. (1992). *Small decencies: Reflections and meditations on being human at work.* New York: HarperCollins.

Cross, A. (1984). *Sweet death, kind death.* New York: E.P. Dutton.

Dima, N. (1990). *Cross cultural communication.* Washington, DC: Institute for the Study of Man.

D'Zurilla, T.J. (1987). Problem-solving therapies. In K.S. Dobson (Ed.), *Handbook of cognitive-behavior therapy.* New York: Guilford Press.

Ellerbee, L. (1995, October 14). I'm gone, but my beliefs live on. *Rocky Mountain News,* p. 61A.

Elliott, D.S. (1997). Editor's introduction. In D.S. Elliott (Ed.), *Blueprints for violence prevention* (Vols. 1–10, pp. 1–14). Boulder: University of Colorado, Institute of Behavioral Science, Center for the Study and Prevention of Violence.

Ellis, A., & Harper, R.A. (1976). *A new guide to rational living.* North Hollywood, CA: Wilshire.

Fadiman, C. (1985). *The Little, Brown book of anecdotes.* Boston: Little, Brown.

Fisher, A. (1995). The ethical problems encountered in psychiatric nursing practice with dangerous mentally ill persons. *Scholarly Inquiry for Nursing Practice: An International Journal, 9,* 193–208.

Fisher, R., Ury, W., & Patton, B. (1991). *Getting to yes.* New York: Penguin Books USA.

Forman, S.G., & Cecil, M.A. (1985). Stress management. In C.A. Maher (Ed.), *Professional self-management: Techniques for special services providers* (pp. 45–63). Baltimore: Paul H. Brookes Publishing Co.

Gardner, J.F., & Chapman, M.S. (1985). *Staff development in mental retardation services: A practical handbook.* Baltimore: Paul H. Brookes Publishing Co.

Gendler, J.R. (1984). *The book of qualities.* Berkeley, CA: Turquoise Mountain Publications.

Giampa, F.L., Walker-Burt, G., & Lamb, D. (Eds.). (1984). *Michigan Department of Mental Health community direct care staff curriculum.* Lansing, MI: Office of Resource Development.

Gilbert, T.F. (1978). *Human competence: Engineering worthy performance.* New York: McGraw-Hill.

Glasser, I. (1981). Prisoners of benevolence: Power versus liberty in the welfare state. In W. Gaylin, I. Glasser, S. Marcus, & D.J. Rothman (Eds.), *Doing good: The limits of benevolence* (pp. 97–170). New York: Pantheon Books.

Goodman, E.G. (1979). *Close to home.* New York: Fawcett Crest.

Goodman, E.G. (1981). *At large.* New York: Summit Books.

Gostin, L.O. (1995). Informed consent, cultural sensitivity, and respect for persons. *JAMA, 274*(10), 844–845.

Greenberg, S.F. (1984). *Stress and the teaching profession.* Baltimore: Paul H. Brookes Publishing Co.

Greenberg, S.F., & Valletutti, P.J. (1980). *Stress and the helping professions.* Baltimore: Paul H. Brookes Publishing Co.

Grimes, C. (1996, March–April). What causes child abuse and neglect. *Mom's & Dad's Magazine* [On-line]. Available: http://www.zipmall.com/moms-causes.htm/

Hamlin, S. (1989). *How to talk so people listen: The real key to job success.* New York: HarperCollins.

Happé, F. (1994). *Autism: An introduction to psychological theory.* Cambridge, MA: Harvard University Press.

Hauck, P.A. (1967). *The rational management of children.* New York: Libra.

Hayakawa, S.I. (1964). *Language in thought and action.* San Diego: Harcourt Brace Jovanovich.

Hayakawa, S.I., Hayakawa, A.R., & MacNeil, R. (1991). *Language in thought and action.* San Diego: Harcourt Brace Jovanovich.

Hromco, J.G., Lyons, J.S., & Nikkel, R.E. (1995). Mental health case management: Characteristics, job function, and occupational stress. *Community Mental Health Journal, 31,* 111–125.

Hulteng, R.J. (1991). The informed consent doctrine in mental health: Legal and ethical traditions. *Psychotherapy in Private Practice, 9*(1), 135–144.

Ivins, M. (1994, September 21). Best solution under circumstances. *Rocky Mountain News,* p. 48A.

Jaffe, D.T., & Scott, C.D. (1984). *From burnout to balance.* New York: McGraw-Hill.

Jeffreys, J.S. (1995). *Coping with workplace change: Dealing with loss and grief.* Menlo Park, CA: Crisp Publishing.

Kabat-Zinn, J. (1990). *Full catastrophe living: Using the wisdom of your body and mind to face stress/pain/illness.* New York: Bantam Doubleday Dell.

Kaye, B.L. (1997). *Up is not the only way.* Palo Alto, CA: Davies-Black Publishing.

Kirsta, A. (1986). *The book of stress survival.* New York: Simon & Schuster.

Kubany, E.S., & Manke, F.P. (1995). Cognitive therapy for trauma-related guilt: Conceptual bases and treatment outlines. *Cognitive and Behavioral Practice, 2,* 27–61.

Kushner, H.S. (1997). *How good do we have to be? A new understanding of guilt and forgiveness.* Boston: Little, Brown.

Lovaas, I.O. (1987). Behavioral treatment and normal educational and intellectual functioning in young autistic children. *Journal of Consulting and Clinical Psychology, 55,* 3–9.

Maher, C.A., & Cook, S.A. (1985). Time management. In C.A. Maher (Ed.), *Professional self-management: Techniques for special services providers* (pp. 23–43). Baltimore: Paul H. Brookes Publishing Co.

Mallon, T. (1984). *A book of one's own: People and their diaries.* New York: Ticknor & Fields.

Manning, S.S., & Gaul, C.E. (1997). The ethics of informed consent: A critical variable in the self-determination of health and mental health clients. *Social Work in Health Care, 25*(3), 103–117.

Martin, J. (1991). *Miss Manners' guide to excruciatingly correct behavior.* New York: Galahad Books.

Mayer, J.J. (1995). *Time management for dummies.* Foster City, CA: IDG Books.

McInerney, J.F. (1985). Authority management. In C.A. Maher (Ed.), *Professional self-management: Techniques for special services providers* (pp. 129–148). Baltimore: Paul H. Brookes Publishing Co.

McKay, M., Davis, M., & Eshelman, E.R. (1995). *The relaxation and stress workbook* (Rev. ed.). Oakland, CA: New Harbinger Publishers.

McMullin, R.C. (1987). *Talk sense to yourself: A guide to cognitive restructuring therapies.* New York: Institute for Rational Emotive Psychotherapy.

Morris, C.D., Niederbuhl, J.M., & Mahr, J.M. (1993). Determining the capability of individuals with mental retardation to give informed consent. *American Journal on Mental Retardation, 98*(2), 263–272.

Murphy, D.J. (1987). How to get along with the boss. *Practical Supervision* (No. 63), 1–3.

Nicoloff, L.K. (1985). *Changing campus environments to support the lesbian/gay experience.* Paper presented at the third annual Campus Ecology Symposium, Pingree Park, CO.

Postman, N., & Weingartner, C. (1969). *Teaching as a subversive activity.* New York: Delacorte Press.

Remen, R.N. (1996). *Kitchen table wisdom: Stories that heal.* New York: Riverhead Books.

Review of *Just in time.* (1986). *Practical Supervision* (No. 52), 5.

Rothman, D.J. (1981a). Afterword. In W. Gaylin, I. Glasser, S. Marcus, & D.J. Rothman (Eds.), *Doing good: The limits of benevolence* (pp. 171–191). New York: Pantheon Books.

Rothman, D.J. (1981b). Introduction. In W. Gaylin, I. Glasser, S. Marcus, & D.J. Rothman, (Eds.), *Doing good: The limits of benevolence* (pp. xi–xii). New York: Pantheon Books.

Rothman, D.J. (1981c). The state as parent: Social policy in the progressive era. In W. Gaylin, I. Glasser, S. Marcus, & D.J. Rothman (Eds.), *Doing good: The limits of benevolence* (pp. 67–96). New York: Pantheon Books.

Sachs, J. (1998). *Break the stress cycle: 10 steps to reducing stress for women.* Holbrook, MA: Adams Media.

Scott, D. (1980). *How to put more time in your life.* New York: Signet.

Scott, G.G. (1990). *Resolving conflict with others and within yourself.* Oakland, CA: New Harbinger Publishers.

Simmons, R. (1997). *Stress: Your questions answered.* Shaftesbury, Dorset, England: Element.

Singleton, J.E. (1993a, September 9). Family-based economies that cheat women. *Rocky Mountain News,* p. 7B.

Singleton, J.E., (1993b, August 12). Poverty: Putting first things first. *Denver Post,* p. 11B.

Tannen, D. (1998, February 27–March 1). How to turn debate into a dialogue. *USA Weekend,* 4–5.

Turkington, C.A. (1998). *Stress management for busy people.* New York: McGraw-Hill.

Ubel, P.A., Zell, M.M., Miller, D.J., Fischer, G.S., Peters-Stefani, D., & Arnold, R.M. (1995). Elevator talk: Observational study of inappropriate comments in a public space. *The American Journal of Medicine, 99,* 190–194.

Vash, C.L. (1984). Evaluation from the client's point of view. In A.S. Halpern & M.J. Fuhrer (Eds.), *Functional assessment in rehabilitation* (pp. 253–267). Baltimore: Paul H. Brookes Publishing Co.

Walker, A. (1989). *The temple of my familiar.* New York: Pocket Books.

Warschaw, T.A. (1980). *Winning by negotiation.* New York: McGraw-Hill.

Woody, R.H. (1984). *The law and the practice of human services.* San Francisco: Jossey-Bass.

World Wide Legal Information Association. (1998). *The WWLIA Legal Dictionary* [On-line]. Available: http://www.wwlia.org/diction.htm/

Ziarnik, J.P. (1980). Developing proactive direct care staff. *Mental Retardation, 18*(6), 289–292.

Zins, J.E. (1985). Work relations management. In C.A. Maher (Ed.), *Professional self-management: Techniques for special services providers* (pp. 105–127). Baltimore: Paul H. Brookes Publishing Co.

USEFUL RESOURCES

Bateson, M.C. (1989). *Composing a life.* New York: Atlantic Monthly Press.

Bepko, C., & Krestan, J. (1990). *Too good for her own good: Searching for self and intimacy in important relationships.* New York: HarperCollins.

Bolles, R.N. (1998). *What color is your parachute? A manual for job-hunters and career changers.* Berkeley, CA: Ten Speed Press.

Bramson, R.M. (1981). *Coping with difficult people.* New York: Ballantine Books.

Cowan, J. (1992). *Small decencies: Reflections and meditations on being human at work.* New York: HarperCollins.

Fisher, R., Ury, W., & Patton, B. (1991). *Getting to yes.* New York: Penguin Books USA.

Hamlin, S. (1989). *How to talk so people listen: The real key to job success.* New York: HarperCollins.

Harp, D., & Feldman, N. (1996). *The three minute mediator.* Oakland, CA: New Harbinger Publishers.

Hirsch, A.S. (1996). *Love your work and success will follow.* New York: John Wiley & Sons.

Kabat-Zinn, J. (1990). *Full catastrophe living: Using the wisdom of your body and mind to face stress/pain/illness.* New York: Bantam Doubleday Dell.

Kaye, B.L. (1997). *Up is not the only way.* Palo Alto, CA: Davies-Black Publishing.

Krannich, R.L., & Krannich, C.R. (1995). *The complete guide to public employment.* Manassas Park, VA: Impact.

Mayer, J.J. (1995). *Time management for dummies.* Foster City, CA: IDG Books.

McGee-Cooper, A., & Trammell, D. (1994). *Time management for unmanageable people.* New York: Bantam Doubleday Dell.

McKay, M., Davis, M., & Eshelman, E.R. (1995). *The relaxation and stress reduction workbook* (Rev. ed.). Oakland, CA: New Harbinger Publishers.

O'Hara, V. (1996). *Five weeks to healing stress.* Oakland, CA: New Harbinger Publishers.

Petras, K., & Petras, R. (1995). *The only job hunting guide you'll ever need* (2nd ed.). New York: Fireside.

Remen, R.N. (1996). *Kitchen table wisdom: Stories that heal.* New York: Riverhead Books.

Saltzman, A. (1991). *Downshifting: Reinventing success on a slower track.* New York: HarperCollins.

Scott, D. (1980). *How to put more time in your life.* New York: Signet.

Scott, G.G. (1990). *Resolving conflict with others and within yourself.* Oakland, CA: New Harbinger Publishers.

Towpov, B. (1997). *The complete idiot's guide to getting along with difficult people.* New York: Alpha Books.

Warschaw, T.A. (1980). *Winning by negotiation.* New York: McGraw-Hill.

INDEX

Page numbers followed by *f* denote figures.

PLACE YOUR ORDER NOW!

FREE shipping and handling on prepaid check orders.

Please send me ____ copy(ies) of **"Human Services? . . . That must be so rewarding"**/Stock #3327/$23.50

___ Bill my institution (P.O. must be attached)

___ Payment enclosed (checks payable: **Brookes Publishing Co.**)

___ VISA ___ MC ___ AMEX Card #: _____

Exp. date: _____ Daytime telephone: _____

Signature: _____

Name: _____

Address: _____

City/State/ZIP: _____

Maryland orders add 5% sales tax. Yours to review 30 days risk free. Price subject to change without notice. Price may be higher outside the United States.

To order
• **send** this form to Brookes Publishing Co., P.O. Box 10624, Baltimore, MD 21285-0624 or **FAX** to (410) 337-8539
• **call** toll-free (8 A.M.–5 P.M. ET) 1-800-638-3775
• or **visit** our web site and order online

Source code: BA13